Concise Historical Atlas of the U.S. Civil War

CONCISE HISTORICAL ATLAS OF THE U.S. CIVIL WAR

Aaron Sheehan-Dean

New York ■ Oxford
OXFORD UNIVERISTY PRESS
2009

Oxford University Press, Inc. publishes works that further Oxford University's
objective of excellence in research, scholarship, and education.

Oxford   New York
Auckland   Cape Town   Dar es Salaam   Hong Kong   Karachi
Kuala Lumpur   Madrid   Melbourne   Mexico City   Nairobi
New Delhi   Shanghai   Taipei   Toronto

With offices in
Argentina   Austria   Brazil   Chile   Czech Republic   France   Greece
Guatemala   Hungary   Italy   Japan   Poland   Portugal   Singapore
South Korea   Switzerland   Thailand   Turkey   Ukraine   Vietnam

Published by Oxford University Press, Inc.
198 Madison Avenue, New York, New York 10016
http://www.oup.com

Library of Congress Cataloging-in-Publication Data

Sheehan-Dean, Aaron Charles.
    Concise historical atlas of the U.S. Civil War / Aaron Sheehan-Dean.
        p. cm.
    Includes bibliographical references and index.
    ISBN 978-0-19-530958-4 (paper)—ISBN 978-0-19-530956-0 (cloth)   1.
United States—History—Civil War, 1861–1865—Campaigns—Maps.   2.
United States—History—Civil War, 1861–1865—Maps.   I. Title.
    G1201.S5S5   2009
    973.7022′3—dc22

                                                    2008036342

9 8 7 6 5 4 3 2 1

Printed in the United States of America
on acid-free paper

For David Wilson,
Deborah Miller, Kim Tryka,

and all those people
who share their expertise with others

CONTENTS

PREFACE

Like all wars, the American Civil War was a geographical conflict. In 1861, the dispute over the future of slavery within the Union produced a crisis over the physical boundaries of national authority. By seceding, southern states repudiated the sovereignty of the federal government and initiated a struggle to create their own country. Once the war began, it was fought on a human scale. Soldiers marched themselves across states and battlefields, supplies traveled in wagons pulled by mules, and most firearms were deadly only when soldiers were close enough to see one other. The geographic reality of the war impressed itself on everyone in America. Soldiers studied roadways, river crossings, and mountain passes. Civilians pored over maps, tracing the routes of their loved ones and the cataclysms about which they read in the newspapers. New places achieved totemic significance—Shiloh, Antietam, Gettysburg, Chickamauga—changing forever Americans' relation to the landscape. For contemporary readers trying to understand the Civil War, mastering the geography of the conflict remains essential.

This atlas assumes that readers need to know where the war transpired, but more important, it uses maps to demonstrate why the war occurred, how it was fought, and why it ended as it did. Maps provide more than just the background, the setting for events; they also help explain those events. This atlas presents a concise and readable geographic account of the Civil War. The major campaigns and the significant battles are represented. In addition, this atlas illustrates most of the important themes of the conflict—from emancipation and occupation to politics and civil liberties—in map form. Just like the physical clash of armies, the patterns of intellectual, economic, and social change and conflict that typified the war possessed geographic characteristics. The Republican and Democratic parties split the North into areas of influence almost as sharply as the Confederacy split from the Union. Within the South, the nature and extent of Union occupation shaped politics in visible ways. Previous scholars have alerted us to some of these trends, but this atlas represents a new attempt to tell these stories with maps rather than words.

Most Civil War atlases reflect the format of the original maps drawn for officers during the war, which focused on comprehensiveness, often including every physical or man-made feature in a given area. This atlas, in contrast, focuses on clarity and readability. The prominent physical features of the landscape are represented and salient details are always included, but the emphasis here has been to craft maps that explain. Of the three types of map included in this atlas—campaign, battle, and data map—the campaign maps illustrate the highest level of movement and operation. For students of the war, the hardest challenge often is mastering the flow of soldiers across regions and states over four years of war. Accordingly, this atlas chronicles the major campaigns in both the eastern and western theaters of war. To fully understand the war, students must also familiarize themselves with the tactics of armies—their movement on the battlefield—and this atlas highlights half a dozen engagements to dramatize the nature of Civil War fighting. The final category of map—

analytical or data map—graphically represents a host of issues that emerged as central during the war itself.

Further differentiating itself, this atlas covers not just the war years but the antebellum and Reconstruction eras as well. Maps of industrialization, agriculture, and politics help establish the context within which Americans initiated and recovered from war. The data maps encourage readers to visualize the geographic distribution of historical information. Where were the largest numbers of factories located before the war? Where was the Democratic Party strongest? Exploring these same questions after the war allows readers to assess the larger impact of the conflict on American development. Maps that focus on the problems of the Reconstruction era—the disputes over civil rights legislation, the growth of sharecropping, and the shape of the new Democratic-Republican political alignments—require us to place these issues in space. In each case, the maps reveal important patterns and force new questions about the outcomes of the war.

Each map is also accompanied by a page of text, which establishes the context within which the information or movement portrayed on the map occurred. In these sections, I have tried to engage with the major themes of the war as they have been identified by scholars, but I do not make direct reference to texts or competing interpretations. Nor should the textual narratives be considered definitive. Behind each of the map-and-text pairings stands a great deal of discussion and debate among historians. My hope here is to introduce readers to the conflict in ways they may not have considered and to open new lines of debate. Readers who are intrigued by particular episodes are encouraged to consult the voluminous literature on the war, where all of the issues raised here are considered in great detail.

The American Civil War occurred over half a continent—the Confederacy occupied more than three-quarters of a million square miles or larger than the space of continental Europe—and conceptualizing this terrain can be a challenge for us today. Most Northerners and Southerners at the time faced the same challenge. They learned a great deal from the reporters who followed Northern armies into Southern towns that rarely made national news in the antebellum period. Most Northern soldiers possessed only a limited knowledge of the places through which they traveled and most Southern soldiers' geographical awareness ended at their own state lines. We have the benefit today of much more ubiquitous geographical representations—all citizens know intuitively the shape of the United States and most can identify the state boundaries. What requires more deliberate attention from today's students of the war is the physical geography of the South—the location and flow of major rivers, the extent and size of southern mountain ranges—and the built infrastructure—most important, roads and railway networks—that shaped the conflict. In both the campaign and battle maps, two aspects of physical geography are emphasized whenever relevant: elevation and waterways. Mountains and rivers formed the major barriers and avenues that shaped the decisions made by commanders about where and whether to engage an enemy. It is important to remember that the Civil War was fought by men who moved on foot (only occasionally on trains) and used draft animals to carry their weapons and material, which made knowledge of gaps in the mountains and the fords over rivers essential.

The first set of maps, on antebellum America, are geared toward making the Civil War explainable, so they are necessarily hindsight driven. This is true of the battle maps as well—they are written to explain the outcome and significance of each campaign, relying on information that the participants did not have. Accordingly, the maps do not convey the confusion or the contingency of most battles. With a few small changes, many of even the most epic battles of the war could have turned out differently. But because these maps are static and because they emphasize explanation of the outcome rather than the process, the reader will derive little of the moment-by-moment unpredictability of Civil War fighting. For that, readers are encouraged to consult the many excellent battle studies currently available (some of which are listed in the selected bibliography at the end of the volume).

It is important to note that not all commanders are represented on the battle or campaign maps. Some campaign maps feature only the names of the commanding general (always written in all capital letters) whereas others also note corps commanders. In terms of symbols (for roads, railroads, rivers, etc.) and labeling, the maps emphasize clarity and readability over comprehensive coverage. The two key criteria were significance and space. Only those people and actions that directly influenced the outcome of a particular campaign or battle are represented on the maps.

The campaign maps feature text boxes that list casualty figures for each side in the major conflicts noted on each map. These figures denote the general scholarly consensus regarding each conflict and represent a combination of those soldiers killed, wounded, or missing in action. The outcomes for missing soldiers varied dramatically in the Civil War. At some engagements, such as Bull Run, most of those listed as missing eventually rejoined their units, whereas at other engagements many of the missing were eventually counted as fatalities. The numbers listed here do not include all of the minor engagements or the many thousands of men who died from disease (either those related to wounds or not) and thus do not total to the commonly accepted figure of 620,000 total war dead.

Last, Federals and Confederates used different naming conventions for the battles, with Northerners using natural features (mostly rivers) and Southerners using nearby towns. Because the Northern names are more widely used in the historical literature, they are adopted here for ease of use and consistency. The towns that Southerners used to designate battles are labeled on all the maps, so readers using the atlas as a supplement to texts that adopt that tradition should be able to follow along.

Americans are accustomed to reading the story of the Civil War in text. The dramatic characters and moments in the story have imposed their own impression on the American language. This atlas is premised on the idea that the conflict can be read with equal profit in maps. The images that follow are complemented by text but they are intended to be read independently. Together, the maps form not a complete history of the conflict but an overview that moves through the main turning points, developments, and issues of the war. A reader should be able to develop a sense of the narrative of the war as well as an explanation for why it ended as it did reading only the maps. I encourage the reader to regard the texts that accompany the maps as provisional, as one possible explanation of what the maps represent. Much more so than written language, maps construct "open" narratives. They allow readers to draw a variety of interpretations. Sometimes, these interpretations may clash with those advanced by the text and I hope readers will generate multiple interpretations themselves. In this respect, maps may be better suited than text to convey the complexity and unpredictability of the American Civil War.

Acknowledgments

This project required skills that I had only in limited supply when I began the work. Most essential has been the help given by those people noted in the book's dedication. At the University of Virginia, Kim Tryka introduced me to much of the digital world. At the University of North Florida, I have relied on the expert advice and ideas of Deb Miller, David Wilson, and Robert Richardson. Robert helped me through a number of difficult points in working with Arc GIS software. Deb helped with Arc as well and guided me through the maze of relationships between the various software programs I used. David's patient instruction in the vagaries of Adobe Illustrator and his willingness to field innumerable e-mails and phone calls has earned him my eternal gratitude and, frankly, made this volume possible. In their willingness and ability to share their expertise with faculty members, they represent the very best traditions of intellectual generosity. I was also fortunate to move next door to a talented artist at the start of this project. Julia DeArriba-Montgomery offered valuable assistance and insight into the nature of color and helped talk me through various design conundrums. Gary Gallagher, as always, offered good advice and encouragement throughout the project. Joan Waugh and Vikki Bynum also answered questions and shared their knowledge. My thanks to them as well as to the students in my Fall 2007 Civil War and Reconstruction course, who gamely evaluated a first draft and provided valuable feedback.

At Oxford, I am grateful to Peter Coveney, who took a chance by inviting me to do this project and another by giving me the liberty to define it as I wished. This project benefited greatly from the involvement of John Challice during the interim between editors. His enthusiasm and probing questions helped me frame my approach. Brian Wheel picked up the assignment and has proved a model editor—patient, encouraging, and always helpful with advice about content and process. I have greatly appreciated the prompt and friendly attention of June Kim, Brad Reina, and, most of all, Laura Lancaster. I am grateful to what felt like a full regiment of anonymous reviewers whom Oxford arranged to evaluate a draft of the manuscript, including Susannah U. Bruce at Sam Houston State University, Mina Carson at Oregon State University, Edward R. Crowther at Adams State College, Sheila Culbert at Dartmouth College, Mackubin Thomas Owens at the U.S. Naval War College, John P. Sample at Rogers State University, and Steven E. Woodworth at Texas Christian University. They saved me many embarrassing errors and offered excellent advice about how to improve the atlas. The book is certainly stronger because of their efforts. At home, my family has made the project more fun than is typical for academic work. Several of the Schrobilgens, Greg and Malachy in particular, read through an early draft of the manuscript and offered insights that strengthened it in several places. Megan was endlessly supportive, providing much needed perspective both on the text and maps and on the challenges of my learning a new way of telling history. Annie and Liam asked countless questions, many of which made it into the atlas. They both drew their own maps and together with Megan showed me the fun and importance of knowing where I am in the world and where I might like to go.

TERMS

Army. The highest operational unit in the Civil War. Each side organized several armies during the war. Some, such as Robert E. Lee's Army of Northern Virginia, lasted for years whereas others had brief lives before being folded back into larger regional armies. They were commanded by major or lieutenant generals and are the units represented on most of the campaign-level maps.

Border. The region between the Union and Confederate states—principally through Missouri, Kentucky, and western Virginia—that became a de facto boundary during the war.

Brigade. The fourth-highest level of organization for Civil War armies. Commanded by brigadier generals, brigades were composed of two to five regiments.

Company. The smallest organizational level of the army, composed of one hundred men, often from the same community. Companies were designated by a letter following their regimental number.

Corps. The second-highest level of organization for Civil War armies, corps are the unit featured on most of the battle maps. They were composed of three or four divisions and had a typical fighting strength of 25,000–40,000. In the Federal armies, corps were designated with roman numerals whereas Confederate corps were named after their commanding general.

Division. The third-highest level of organization for Civil War armies. Commanded by brigadier or major generals, divisions were composed of two to four brigades.

Free blacks. The designation for people of color who were free before the Civil War.

Freedpeople. The designation for people of color freed during the Civil War.

Hard war. The policy adopted gradually by the Union Army that targeted the Confederacy's logistical resources. Epitomized by William T. Sherman's campaigns in Georgia and South Carolina and Philip Sheridan in Virginia's Shenandoah Valley, the policy authorized the destruction of any materials that supported the Confederacy's ability to wage war.

Logistics. The aspects of military operations dealing with the acquisition, movement, and distribution of supplies for an army.

Material. The equipment, apparatus, and supplies used by armies.

Regiment. The basic operational unit of Civil War armies. Regiments were raised in specific communities, denoted by a number and a state designation—the 2nd Rhode Island, the 10th Mississippi—and commanded by a colonel or lieutenant colonel. They were typically composed of ten companies of one hundred men apiece, but disease, transfer, and casualties often reduced the fighting strength of individual regiments down to several hundred men.

Shenandoah Valley, Virginia. The Shenandoah Valley has its own unique lexicon. Because the Blue Ridge and Allegheny Mountains rise in elevation from north to south, "Upper Valley" designates the more southern portion and "Lower Valley" denotes the northern reaches.

Strategy. The aspect of military operations dealing with the grand movement of armies over a period of several months or across large geographic areas.

Tactics. The aspect of military operations dealing with the arrangement and movement of small units on a battlefield.

FULL STRENGTH ORGANIZATION OF CIVIL WAR MILITARY UNITS

Army
60,000–
100,000 men

Corps
24,000–
36,000 men

Division
9,000–
12,000 men

Brigade
3000 men

Regiment
1000 men

Company
100 men

⸸ = **100 men**

Key to Symbols Used in Maps

→	Confederate Advance	⬟	Confederate Port
→	Union Advance	⬟	Union Port
⇢	Confederate Retreat		Union Blockading Force
⇢	Union Retreat	✕	Northern Draft Riots
✹	Battle	✕	Confederate Deserter Conflicts
●	Town	⤬	Native American Conflicts
✝	Church	🌿	Wetlands
	Forested area		One Army Division
	Elevated Terrain		Guerilla Conflicts
	Areas of Copperhead Support		Artillery Emplacement
	Areas of Unionist Support	▲	Contraband Camp
—	Railroad Lines		Site of Confederate surrender
	Confederate Defensive Line		
	Union Defensive Line		

CONCISE HISTORICAL ATLAS OF THE U.S. CIVIL WAR

1 U.S. TERRITORIAL GROWTH

American expansion, from the original thirteen colonies to the continental nation that it had become by the mid-nineteenth century, required deliberate action on the part of the federal government. Although the annexation of western lands is often viewed as inevitable, each stage of the process required diplomatic finesse, military force, and considerable demographic and economic pressure applied by white settlers seeking cheaper lands. Each acquisition generated conflict within the United States as pro- and antiexpansion forces clashed over the necessity and purpose of territorial growth.

The largest single acquisition—Jefferson's purchase of the Louisiana Territory from the French in 1803—happened against the wishes of many legislators within Jefferson's own party. His supporters had preached fiscal austerity and small government in their campaigns against the Federalists. The deficit spending required to make the Louisiana Purchase rankled old guard conservatives, but the longer-term result of Jefferson's decision to assume American control over the three-quarters of a million acre French holdings to the west of the Mississippi River, just like the acquisition of land as a result of the Mexican-American War forty years later, was to exacerbate friction between pro- and antislavery forces within the country.

Representation in the U.S. Senate was evenly balanced between slave and free states until 1820, when the admission of Missouri threatened to upset the system. A long and rancorous congressional session yielded a compromise that satisfied few on either side: Maine was admitted as a free state, Missouri as a slave state, and the Missouri Compromise Line was struck. All land within the Louisiana Purchase territory north of Missouri's southern boundary (the 36′ 30° line of latitude) would be organized as free states and all land south of that line would be organized as slave states. Despite temporarily preserving sectional balance within the Senate, the plan left both pro- and antislavery activists feeling as though the government had turned against them. The mere fact of such open and hostile debate worried many observers; Thomas Jefferson proclaimed the debates the "death knell" for the union.

Despite Jefferson's dire warning, the union remained intact, weathering the Nullification Crisis in 1832 and struggles over Texas in 1846–1848. A far greater challenge was the disposition of lands acquired during the war with Mexico. By 1848, the United States had assumed control of most of today's contemporary Southwest and Pacific Northwest. The question of whether to apply the Missouri Compromise Line to this new territory or create some new standard was brought to light by the introduction of a proposal by Pennsylvania Democrat David Wilmot that all land seized in the war with Mexico would be free territory (following Mexico's standing law at the time, which forbade the ownership of slaves). Antislavery legislators appended this language to a wide variety of bills in the years after the war, continually forcing the question of the expansion of slavery into the public spotlight. Voting on the Wilmot Proviso blurred party lines, as southerners expressed outrage over what they perceived would be a violation of their constitutional right to emigrate with their property within the country. In 1854, Democrats pushed through the Kansas-Nebraska Act, which repealed the Missouri Compromise and instituted "popular sovereignty" in its place, an awkward policy that allowed territorial residents to decide on the status of slavery before statehood. The bill's passage inspired the creation of the Republican Party and utterly failed to quell the controversy, which dominated American politics, and the lives of settlers, through the 1850s. The process of territorial growth, lauded by all parties as a natural expression of American democracy, generated the most serious threat to that democracy.

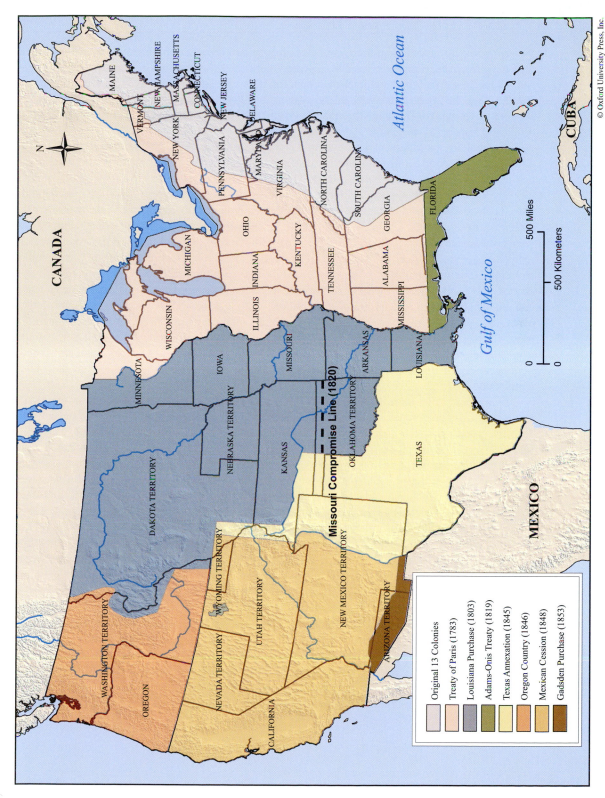

CANADA

Atlantic Ocean

MAINE
NEW HAMPSHIRE
VERMONT
MASSACHUSETTS
CONNECTICUT
NEW YORK
NEW JERSEY
DELAWARE
PENNSYLVANIA
MARYLAND
VIRGINIA
NORTH CAROLINA
SOUTH CAROLINA
GEORGIA
FLORIDA

MICHIGAN
OHIO
KENTUCKY
TENNESSEE
ALABAMA
MISSISSIPPI

WISCONSIN
ILLINOIS
INDIANA
MINNESOTA
IOWA
MISSOURI
ARKANSAS
LOUISIANA

Gulf of Mexico

CUBA

DAKOTA TERRITORY
NEBRASKA TERRITORY
KANSAS
OKLAHOMA TERRITORY
Missouri Compromise Line (1820)

TEXAS

MEXICO

WASHINGTON TERRITORY
OREGON
NEVADA TERRITORY
CALIFORNIA
UTAH TERRITORY
WYOMING TERRITORY
NEW MEXICO TERRITORY
ARIZONA TERRITORY

N

500 Miles
500 Kilometers
0
0

Original 13 Colonies
Treaty of Paris (1783)
Louisiana Purchase (1803)
Adams-Onis Treaty (1819)
Texas Annexation (1845)
Oregon Country (1846)
Mexican Cession (1848)
Gadsden Purchase (1853)

2 SLAVEHOLDING IN THE UNITED STATES

Historians are nearly unanimous today in identifying slavery as the fundamental cause of the Civil War. They disagree over how slavery generated the conflicts that drove the nation to war—some argue that the most important manifestations of slavery's divisiveness were in political conflict over the status of slavery in the western territories; others stress the economic conflict between advocates for free and slave labor; and still others focus on the moral and cultural rift that developed, especially within the evangelical churches.

Slaveholding in America was a dynamic practice; it differed by time and across space. By the mid-nineteenth century, the vast majority of African Americans who lived in the South (three and a half out of four million) were held as slaves. Their lives were shaped largely by the decisions of their masters, who had nearly complete dominion over them. In 1860, 25 percent of southern households owned slaves, down from 30 percent in 1850. Although only the top 10 percent of slaveowners held more than twelve slaves, a majority of slaves worked on plantations. Slaves in the antebellum South were used largely to assist with the growth and harvesting of a set of profitable export crops—principally cotton, tobacco, rice, and sugar—but they also worked in households, factories, mines, mills, and cities. The high numbers of slaves rented out on yearly contracts in southern urban centers created new challenges for owners and the state as both sought to maintain the system of violence and force that confined African Americans to slavery. Although slaves represented a larger proportion of the total population in Lower South states, in terms of absolute numbers, Virginia contained the most with nearly half a million bondsmen. In all parts of the South, investment in slave labor returned a handsome profit. The American South produced 70 percent of the world's supply of cotton in 1860, the majority of that going to Great Britain and France, who were building empires based on their textile trade.

In response to an increasingly public criticism of slaveholding within the North in the 1830s and to the resistance of slaves themselves, southern polemicists articulated a vision of slavery as a "positive good," a system that delivered African slaves to benevolent Christian owners. This contrasted markedly with the perspective of the Revolutionary Generation, who imagined that slavery would "whither away." Instead, slavery flourished not only in the Cotton Belt of central Georgia, Alabama, and Mississippi but also along the Atlantic Seaboard, in central and western Tennessee, and central Kentucky. Slaveholders dominated local, state, and national government posts and slavery permeated all aspects of antebellum southern life. It gave unique shape to the system of honor among white men and structured the class relations among those men as well.

The movement to abolish slavery grew out of Enlightenment beliefs and began in earnest in late eighteenth-century Great Britain. Spurred by religious reforms associated with the Second Great Awakening, American abolitionists began advocating for an end to slavery from outside the political system. Frederick Douglass and William Lloyd Garrison led the official movement while Harriet Beecher Stowe's novel *Uncle Tom's Cabin* alerted hundreds of thousands of readers to their own complicity through the national government's sanction of the practice. Abolitionists were joined in their critique of slavery by advocates for free labor, a doctrine that celebrated the moral, economic, and political righteousness of independent work. Abolitionists alienated most white southerners with their increasingly strident rhetoric but made little headway winning over northerners in the years before the war. Instead, most northern opposition to slavery developed out of concern about the effect of the institution on American democracy and the national economy; most white northerners cared little for African Americans as people.

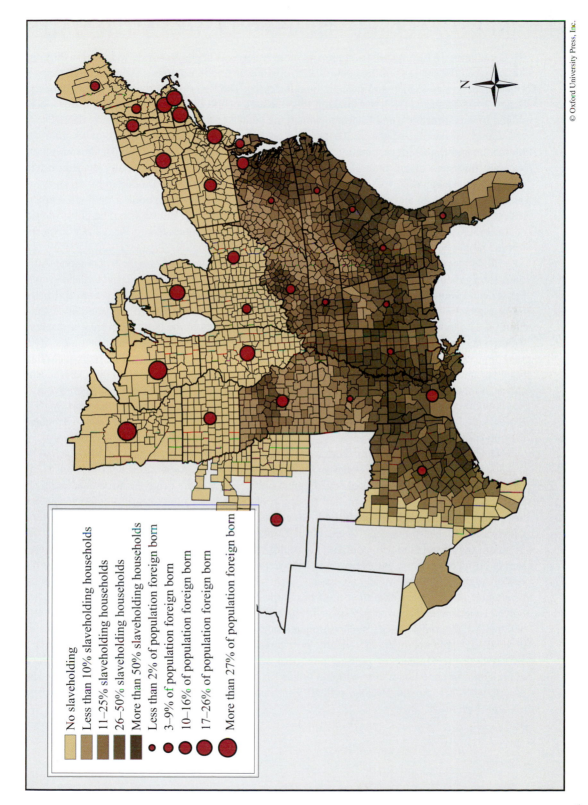

N

Legend:

No slaveholding
Less than 10% slaveholding households
11–25% slaveholding households
26–50% slaveholding households
More than 50% slaveholding households
Less than 2% of population foreign born
3–9% of population foreign born
10–16% of population foreign born
17–26% of population foreign born
More than 27% of population foreign born

3 INDUSTRIAL ESTABLISHMENTS IN THE UNITED STATES

Through the 1840s and 1850s, more and more Americans began to notice and discuss differences between the sections of the country. The obvious distinction between slave and free states provided an easy way to map and explain the differences. The Republican ideology of free labor positioned itself against slave labor, making this one area of life with a clear boundary. But a host of shared beliefs, practices, and traditions united the people of the country at the same time. The Second Great Awakening of the 1830s inspired an outpouring of faith all across the country. The Methodist and Baptist denominations, in particular, developed out of the enthusiasm spurred on by itinerant ministers of the time. Although northerners emphasized the necessity of demonstrating one's faith through good works (including, in some cases, abolition) and southerners stressed the individual nature of sin and redemption, the evangelical movement drew people from both regions together with a shared language and a shared vision of the purpose of human life. The political system of the 1830s and 1840s likewise drew Americans together. Democrats and Whigs in both sections formed alliances with fellow party members from North and South.

Moderates in both sections stressed these shared values as they sought to counteract the inflammatory rhetoric of abolitionists and fire-eaters. What the moderates could not explain away was the growing economic differences between the two sections. The North's increasing, and increasingly rapid, industrialization resulted in built environments that differed substantially from the South's. The most telling difference was that even small towns in the North sported a wide array of shops, many carrying goods from around the world. Northerners proudly identified their style of economic development as the vanguard of modernity, while southerners sought a more complicated fusion of new forms of capitalism with the old tradition of slavery. Beginning in the 1820s, northern states and localities had invested heavily in canals and railroads, something less imperative for the South with its system of natural waterways that already delivered goods to coastal markets. Northerners' early practice with corporations and stock and bond investments gave them an advantage as they diversified their economy in the second and third decades of the nineteenth century.

The result was that by 1860, there were as many industrial establishments in the North as there were industrial workers in the South and it did not require close familiarity with the census to see the difference. Northern industrial development was heaviest in the urban northeast and parts of the Midwest. New York, Philadelphia, and Boston could each boast hundreds of manufacturing establishments while second-tier cities built along canal or railroad lines—like Buffalo, Pittsburgh, Cleveland, and Detroit—raced to catch up. Northern industrialization was both broad and deep. Southern industrialization, in contrast, was more localized, often around natural resources like the iron deposits in Virginia, or developed as an extension of slave production, as with the cotton factories of Augusta. With the steady increase of slave labor each year, southerners had little incentive to mechanize production within their most profitable export areas—staple crops. By the 1850s, northerners' investments began to pay off, with lucrative finished goods, such as furniture and textiles, and heavy industrial products, such as iron and steel, entering world markets. Not only did this more diversified development strategy yield a more dynamic antebellum economy, it was also much better suited to the demands of fighting a modern war. Northerners could shift resources invested in commercial or state bonds into national bonds for the war effort with little difficulty, while southerners, with their capital invested primarily in slaves and land, fought the war on a much weaker economic platform.

1 or fewer industrial establishments per 1000 residents

2–4 industrial establishments per 1000 residents

5–7 industrial establishments per 1000 residents

8 or more industrial establishments per 1000 residents

4 AGRICULTURAL PRODUCTIVITY IN THE UNITED STATES

Although most southerners understood the deficit they faced regarding industrial development, few would have recognized the same dynamic in comparisons of regional agricultural production. Since colonial times, the South had been known around the world as an agricultural paradise and powerhouse—fertile soil, a long growing season, easy access to water for irrigation or shipping, and a wealth of arable land led observers to envision unlimited success in farm-based markets. With the exception of slumps in the tobacco market in the late seventeenth and eighteenth centuries, the South had generally lived up to expectation. Southern farmers, many of them large planters relying on slave labor, produced valuable crops distributed around the globe. By the mid-nineteenth century, the dominant products of the South were cotton, rice, tobacco, sugar, indigo, and corn. The first five were the staple crops farmed explicitly for export to Europe whereas the sixth (like other grains farmed in smaller amounts) was intended for domestic, often local, consumption. The expansion of white settler control into the fertile lands of northern Georgia, Alabama, and Mississippi once controlled by Native Americans in the 1820s and 1830s opened a new era in the southern farm economy. Cotton production skyrocketed, racing to meet the demand of British and French empires built on a trade in textiles, and with it southern fortunes. The success of the southern agricultural model offers one explanation for secession—southern farmers who felt threatened by the northern model of free labor had much to lose from the end of the slavery.

Northerners, by contrast, had little success with the staple crops that enriched southern farmers—tobacco, sugar, and indigo could not be grown profitably in the northern climate. Forced to diversify, northerners developed dynamic regional economies, producing goods for local consumption in markets that with the aid of the railroad soon stretched across whole states. Using new technologies like the horse-drawn reaper—built by a Virginian, Cyrus McCormick, who moved to Chicago to produce and market his machine—they also generated an increasingly lucrative market in wheat production. Requiring less labor than corn, wheat could be grown by families in large volumes and it fetched increasingly high prices in South American and European markets in the late antebellum period. The Crimean War of the mid-1850s spurred demand in Europe for American grain and northern farmers benefited. Comparing the total value of agricultural products by county highlights the North's surprising success. Wheat production generated real wealth across broad swaths of the North, especially upstate New York, Connecticut, Massachusetts, and parts of New Jersey and Pennsylvania. The lesson for northerners in this experience was that free labor was viable and could power a national economy to lasting success.

The distribution of agricultural resources and productivity had profound importance during the war itself. During the conflict, Southerners struggled to shift their export-based economy over to one geared around domestic consumption. This required prohibiting the production of cotton beyond what was necessary for war- and home-related enterprises. Sugar and tobacco likewise had little value beyond their immediate domestic use. But with prices for these goods escalating in Europe thanks to the Northern blockade, Southern farmers found strong incentives to secretly produce these crops for export on blockade runners. During the war, the Confederate government pleaded, cajoled, and coerced Southern farmers to focus on foodstuffs, whereas Northern farmers could produce wheat to feed both citizens and soldiers even with the loss of manpower to the armies. The highly visible advantages of the southern economy before the war became liabilities once the war commenced and the depth of northern resources became one of the explanations for the North's eventual victory.

Less than $2,500 in total agricultural production

$2,501–$10,000 in total agricultural production

$10,001–$25,000 in total agricultural production

$25,001–$50,000 in total agricultural production

$50,001+ in total agricultural production

Note: Agricultural production is the value of all Orchard and Market Garden crops as listed in the 1860 Census.

5 U.S. PRESIDENTIAL ELECTION

When Abraham Lincoln won the 1860 presidential election, it represented a significant accomplishment for the Republican Party, which had been in existence for less than a decade. By far the most successful of the various opposition parties that flourished in the nineteenth century, the Republicans built out of the ruins of the Whig Party and the brief Nativist Movement a formidable political movement based on the idea of free labor. This philosophy emphasized the possibility, even necessity, of upward mobility, which in turn ensured that landless men would participate responsibly in the political system, the chief fear that kept European nations from endorsing universal manhood suffrage. Abraham Lincoln stood as a living personification of the promise of economic advancement, beginning adult life as a "rail splitter" and maturing into a successful lawyer and politician. After a single term in Congress, Lincoln had retired from politics, only to be drawn back in by the fight over the Kansas-Nebraska Act.

Rather than streamlining the process for organizing western territories, the congressional action merely shifted the fight from the halls of the Capitol to the plains of Kansas, where pro- and antislavery settlers battled in increasingly violent and bloody conflicts throughout the late 1850s. Building on northern concern over the vigor of the proslavery response in the West and the enormous population growth in the North over previous decades, Republicans created a wholly sectional party. During the campaign Lincoln spoke to northern audiences and did not even appear on the ballots in most southern districts. As predicted, Lincoln ran strongly in the upper sections of the North and, surprisingly, in many lower North districts as well. He won just over 40 percent of the popular vote, a clear plurality but a low enough total to ensure continuing attacks from opponents throughout his presidency. Lincoln won enough electoral college votes to capture the office outright, frustrating conservatives of both parties who hoped to have the election sent into the House, where a compromise candidate would have been selected.

Opposing Lincoln were John Breckinridge, a southern Democrat; Stephen Douglas, a northern Democrat; and John Bell, of the newly minted Constitutional Union Party. Breckinridge and Douglas emerged from the collapse of the Democratic Party. The Democrats unwisely chose to open their party convention in Charleston, where Deep South representatives abandoned the meeting because northern members refused to add a provision ensuring the protection of slavery in the federal territories. Northerners reconvened in Baltimore and elected Douglas, a conservative northerner who professed to be agnostic on the question of slavery's expansion. Breckinridge, nominated in a separate meeting of southern Democrats, pledged to protect slavery in the territories. John Bell, put forward by former Whigs, asserted only a love of the union and respect for the Constitution. He won the support of cautious voters in the Upper South, including much of Virginia and Kentucky. Breckinridge campaigned in and won most of the Deep South precincts. Douglas, alone among the candidates, campaigned in both sections and preached the gospel of union against those on either side who would divide the union. He won only one state outright: the seven electoral votes of Missouri. A handful of districts elected conservative electors dedicated to a "fusion" of Democratic and Republican values without a specific party identity.

The election produced divisions that seemingly mirror the later divisions of the Civil War, but upon close examination it proves to be a poor guide to attitudes on secession. Northern Democrats retained their faith, obeying even when party managers insisted that they support Breckinridge (usually as a result of personality conflicts among the various Democratic supporters at the local level). Southerners divided along a number of lines, and even Breckinridge himself never suggested that failure in the election would constitute grounds for secession. The first successful Republican election ended a long era of Democratic dominance and initiated a series of events that culminated in civil war.

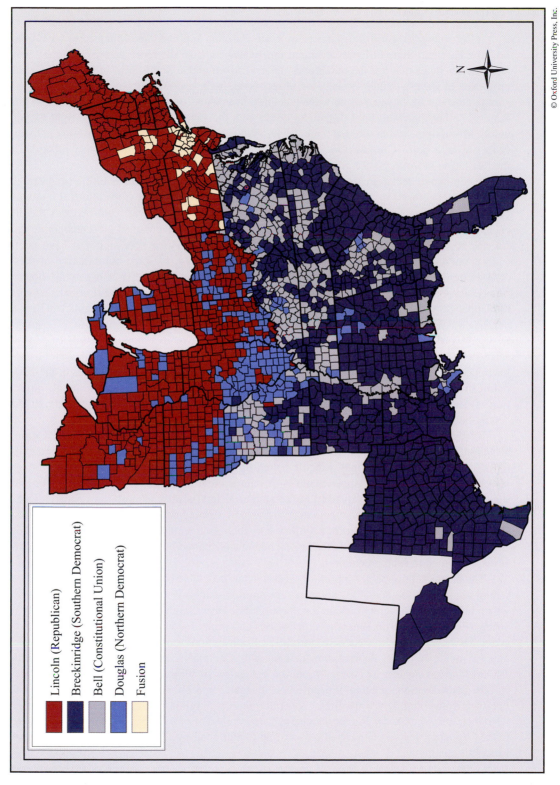

N

Lincoln (Republican)
Breckinridge (Southern Democrat)
Bell (Constitutional Union)
Douglas (Northern Democrat)
Fusion

6 SECESSION

On December 20, 1860, delegates from South Carolina approved an ordinance of secession and the Palmetto State officially declared independence. Like the representatives of the six other Deep South states that left the union over the next two months, South Carolinians emphasized the protection of slavery in their explanation of secession. In their view, Lincoln's election presaged the commencement of "a war [to] be waged against slavery until it shall cease throughout the United States." Rather than wait until despotism descended, the state exercised its stated right to exit the union. Mississippi, which seceded three weeks later, echoed South Carolina's reasoning in listing its causes of secession. "Our position," the Mississippi delegates began, "is thoroughly identified with the institution of slavery—the greatest material interest of the world."

In contrast to decisive action of Deep South states, the majority of slaveholding states (eight of fifteen) either refused to consider the issue of secession or organized conventions dominated by conservatives who began lengthy deliberations. Historians disagree over what explains the differences between the two regions. Many Upper South southerners maintained close economic, political, and social connections with the North. Their hesitancy to endorse secession may have stemmed from economic interest, fraternal sentiment, political alliances, or some combination of these or other issues. Regardless of the mix of motives, it is important to distinguish between the support for immediate secession in the Lower South with the widespread support for conditional secession in the Upper South. A majority of Upper South citizens believed in the constitutionality of secession but they did not feel that Lincoln's election alone justified the act. Instead, they waited, hoping that tensions would subside before either the North or the Lower South committed a rash act that would force them to choose sides. Lincoln sought to placate the remaining slave states but stood firm on his opposition to the expansion of slavery in the territories—one of the cornerstones of the new Republican Party—and rejected the right of secession categorically. Lincoln argued that the preservation of democracy hinged on a repudiation of secession; the world must know, he wrote, that there "could be no appeal from the ballot to the bullet."

By the firing on Fort Sumter in Charleston Harbor on April 12, the northernmost group of slaveholding states—Missouri, Kentucky, Maryland, and Delaware—had rejected secession. But immediately following the fight, Lincoln called up 75,000 militia from the states, and the tier of slave states known as the "Upper South"—Arkansas, Tennessee, North Carolina, and Virginia—seceded. These states stood squarely in the path of federal armies assembling to march to South Carolina and their support was essential to the new Confederate States of America (organized February 4, 1861). Virginia, North Carolina, and Tennessee would together send 40 percent of the Confederacy's soldiers. They held the largest manufacturing facilities and a majority of the southern acreage devoted to food production.

The question of popular support for secession has bedeviled historians for generations. Reliable voting records on the actual question of secession exist in only a handful of Upper South states, which held popular referendums on the question. For Deep South states, historians must rely upon voting for delegates to the secession conventions as a proxy for support of secession. Even in those states where secession was endorsed strongly by conventions, popular voting reveals the fluid nature of public opinion. Prosecession delegates to Georgia's convention, for instance, garnered 50,000 votes as against 37,000 for prounion delegates. In Virginia the populace initially favored careful consideration, sending 106 prounion delegates and only 46 prosecession delegates to its February convention. Even the final convention vote in Virginia reflected the divided loyalties of residents; it passed 88–55. Rather than being foreordained, secession was a historical response, motivated by equal parts emotion and reason, and conditioned by the events and attitudes following Lincoln's election.

N

New York

Pennsylvania

Maryland

Delaware

Virginia
April 17, 1861

North Carolina
May 20, 1861

South Carolina
December 20, 1860

Florida
January 19, 1861

Georgia
January 19, 1861

Michigan

Ohio

Kentucky

Tennessee
May 6, 1861

Alabama
January 10, 1861

Indiana

Wisconsin

Illinois

Missouri

Mississippi
January 9, 1861

Iowa

Arkansas
May 6, 1861

Louisiana
January 25, 1861

Kansas

Oklahoma Territory

Texas
February 1, 1861

Note: Measure of support for secession is based on final convention votes.

States and Territories not seceding

Slaveholding states not seceding

Moderate support for secession

Strong support for secession

Very strong support for secession

7 TRANSPORTATION ROUTES IN THE SOUTH

Like several aspects of antebellum life that had been assets in the antebellum period, southern rivers became liabilities during the war. From the colonial period on, southern farmers had relied upon the access granted by southern rivers to ship their products to markets. Unlike the North, where many producers had to haul their goods via wagon (and later railroad), a network of broad rivers ran south or east from the heart of southern agricultural lands to the Gulf of Mexico or the Atlantic coast. The Mississippi was the largest and the most well-known of these byways. Most of the nation's wealthiest planters lined its banks in southern Mississippi and Louisiana. Their location was not accidental. New Orleans, located sixty miles upstream from the river's mouth, channeled goods into ships destined for ports around the world. The same was true of the James River, which ran into Richmond, the Cape Fear, which ended at Wilmington, the Savannah, and dozens of other tributaries that delivered freight to worldwide ports. The rivers were the first targets of invasion, identified by Union general-in-chief Winfield Scott in his famously derided but prescient "Anaconda Plan," which advised control of southern waterways and the coast as the means to subdue the rebellion. Despite the public skepticism that greeted Scott's plan, northern military planners and generals alike put their troops on ships and headed into the South on its rivers. Control of the Mississippi became a preeminent goal of the Union and when accomplished in 1863, effectively split the Confederacy in half.

The other major means of transportation, of people and goods, in the mid-nineteenth century was the railroad. The technological challenges of building trains and roads were only surmounted in the 1830s, and Americans pursued railroad construction after this with a fervor. Businessmen and farmers in all sections sponsored development by chartering railroad corporations. This process moved faster in the antebellum North, and visitors to the South often derided the lack of investment made in the "iron horse." These visitors often failed to appreciate that waterways already provided free access and also underestimated the enthusiasm of southerners for new technologies. In hundreds of small southern towns, local leaders raised money and expectations for the promise of the railroad. Although the highest hopes were seldom fulfilled, southerners built an extensive network of railroads, many in the 1850s. Most important, in terms of waging the war, was the network of east-west lines that tied seaboard states with those in the interior. By 1860, railroad networks connected Virginia with Tennessee and North Carolina; South Carolina with Georgia; Georgia with Tennessee and Alabama; and Mississippi with Texas, Tennessee, and Arkansas. The full network of these roads meant that Southern commanders could channel supplies and men within the region much more efficiently than would have been possible even a decade before. Consequently, Northern commanders targeted southern railroads, particularly the strategic interchanges in places like Corinth, Nashville, Chattanooga, Atlanta, Memphis, and Petersburg.

Railroads also served a tactical interest in specific engagements, usually benefiting the side that arrayed its troops most advantageously. The goal of every commander trained at West Point (which included the vast majority on both sides) was to secure "interior lines." This meant arranging troops in convex shapes that allowed them to be shifted quickly between points as needed, as demonstrated most famously by Joseph Johnston during the Battle of First Manassas, when his men provided a critical boost to the Confederates' afternoon counterattack.

Atlantic Ocean

N

OHIO

INDIANA

Ohio River

Missouri River

Arkansas River

Mississippi River

Tennessee River

Richmond
Petersburg
Norfolk
Washington, D.C.
Baltimore
Raleigh
Charlotte
Florence
Charleston
Savannah
Jacksonville
Danville
Lynchburg
Charleston
Parkersburg
Columbia
Augusta
Macon
Tallahassee
Atlanta
Chattanooga
Talladega
Montgomery
Knoxville
Lexington
Cincinnati
Louisville
Nashville
Decatur
Corinth
Mobile
New Orleans
Evansville
Saint Louis
Cape Girardeau
Memphis
Jackson
Baton Rouge
Bentonville
Little Rock
Shreveport
Sabine Pass
Houston

Cities
Railroad Lines
Rivers

15

Geography played a crucial role in shaping the Civil War. The Appalachian Mountains divided the Eastern and Western theaters of war, while the Mississippi River defined the westernmost Trans-Mississippi theater. The mountains proved to be significant barriers to the movement of troops, which kept the theaters generally distinct in terms of personnel and action. Southern rivers further defined the conflict. In Virginia, the Rapidan-Rappahannock River system, which flowed past Fredericksburg to the Atlantic, became the de facto boundary between Union and Confederate control for much of the war. Other southern rivers served as avenues channeling Union troops into the region.

In general, geography favored the Confederacy. The sheer size of the new nation—some three-quarters of a million square miles or larger than continental Europe—weighed in its favor. Military leaders on both sides understood the advantages of defending as opposed to conquering territory, though Jefferson Davis's pledge to protect all Confederate territory created the grounds for disillusionment among westerners when this proved impossible. The 3,000-mile coastline only complicated factors further, and in the early months of the war, Abraham Lincoln called for a blockade of Southern ports. Although the blockade gained effectiveness through the war, Southerners initially rebuffed Union plans of encircling the whole Confederacy as ridiculous. Another geographic factor—the mountains running down the eastern states—frustrated Union efforts to exploit their numerical advantages. Although the Confederacy could wage a strictly defensive war, victory for the North required invasion and conquest, a process greatly complicated by the size and variety of southern terrain.

Most of the major battles of the war were concentrated within sections of the Eastern and Western theaters themselves. In the East, the majority of fighting happened on the axis between Richmond and Washington. Four years of struggle for the national capitals reduced much of central Virginia to a wasteland. Small, rural towns—Orange, Culpeper, Gordonsville—became emblazoned on American memories. A similar struggle for control of central Tennessee preoccupied both sides for much of 1862 and 1863. Citizens of these regions experienced the sustained power of war more directly than people in any other area and their plight was absorbed vicariously through newspaper reporting in both North and South. It is important to note that the concentration of major battles in eastern Virginia and central Tennessee produced markedly different war experiences for the people of those sections compared with Southerners located in interior sections who only witnessed limited Union invasion and much of that late in the war. This difference manifested itself in stronger support for central government measures to win the war among those most directly affected.

In the East, forays into Maryland and Pennsylvania marked the departures from Virginia battlefields, while in the West, armies of both nations fought through parts of Kentucky, Arkansas, and Missouri. The capture of Vicksburg in July 1863 put the whole Mississippi River into Union hands and isolated the Trans-Mississippi theater for the remainder of the war. The North could rightly claim this as a victory because it denied important sustenance, especially Texas beef, to Confederate armies farther to the east.

Atlantic Ocean

200 Miles

200 Kilometers

© Oxford University Press, Inc.

NJ
DE
MD
PA
VIRGINIA
OHIO
INDIANA
KENTUCKY
TENNESSEE
NORTH CAROLINA
SOUTH CAROLINA
GEORGIA
ALABAMA
MISSISSIPPI
FLORIDA
LOUISIANA
MISSOURI
ARKANSAS
TEXAS

Gettysburg
Manassas
Fredericksburg
Spotsylvania
Cold Harbor
Richmond
Petersburg
Durham
Fayetteville
Fort Fisher
Antietam
Winchester
Front Royal
Wilderness
Appomattox
Charleston
Savannah
Columbia
Olustee
Atlanta
Knoxville
Chattanooga
Chickamauga
Frankfort
Perryville
Stones River
Nashville
Fort Henry
Fort Donelson
New Madrid
Island No. 10
Shiloh
Corinth
Memphis
Mobile
Jackson
Vicksburg
Port Hudson
New Orleans
Wilson's Creek
Pea Ridge

Battlefields

Elevation

Less than 590 feet
591–1,824 feet
1,825–3,225 feet
Higher than 3,226 feet

17

9 VIRGINIA

The first year of fighting in Virginia foreshadowed the pattern of the war as a whole for the next four years. Confederates established a clear defensive line across central Virginia and rebuffed the high-profile Union campaign toward Richmond before it even crossed the Rappahannock River. In the West, U.S. forces had considerably more success. Exploiting their numerical advantage and the Unionist leanings of some civilians, Federal forces penetrated deep into the western reaches of the state.

After the brief bombardment of Fort Sumter in South Carolina, all eyes turned to Virginia, where the two capitals stood less than one hundred miles apart. Men from all over the South poured into Richmond through the summer, eager to participate in what they expected would be a short and glorious rout of the North. Northerners likewise eagerly entered the fray, with most states sending thousands more soldiers than Lincoln had requested in his initial mobilization of the country's militia to suppress what he termed an "insurrection." General Irvin McDowell, an old veteran of the U.S. regular army, organized the fresh recruits gathered around Washington, D.C. By midsummer, Confederate forces had positioned themselves across a broad arc in central Virginia. Although Northern military planners felt the green troops needed more drill and instruction, Lincoln responded to public pressure and commanded McDowell to start his troops for Richmond.

McDowell's soldiers encountered Confederate regiments beginning on July 18, but the main clash of the two armies occurred on July 21 near Manassas, where P. G. T. Beauregard's Confederates had been bolstered by the forces of Theophilus Holmes, and signaled the true start of the Civil War. Union forces pressed across a small stream, known locally as Bull Run, and experienced success through the morning, forcing Confederate units to a final stand on Henry House Hill. In one of the war's many contingent tipping points, McDowell allowed the tired Northern troops to pause their offensive as the Confederates, rallied by Confederate General Thomas Jonathan Jackson (soon to be christened "Stonewall" for his actions here), pushed back. Reinforced by Joseph Johnston's men, who were among the first soldiers delivered to a battlefield by train, the Confederates overpowered the Federals. The Northern ranks retreated and then broke, with men scattering their belongings in a hasty and unplanned retreat. Congressmen and spectators who had journeyed to Manassas for the day were caught up in the dangerous flight back to Washington. The equally disorganized but nonetheless victorious Confederates celebrated their triumph. For the Union, it was an embarrassing defeat. The scale of bloodshed surprised both sides; the 3,400 casualties made it the deadliest land battle in North America to that date.

The North's success in Virginia in 1861 came when General George Bertrand McClellan deftly maneuvered his forces deep into the state's western regions. Union forces pushed back Confederates at Grafton, a junction town for the strategic Baltimore & Ohio Railroad; Philippi, where the Rebels' hasty retreat was dubbed the "Philippi Races"; and Beverly, where the Confederate general Robert S. Robert Garnett was killed. The result of the campaign brought sanctuary for Unionist civilians in the West; a boost for McClellan's reputation in Washington; and disappointment for Confederates, who watched as incompetent generals fought among themselves and ceded valuable territory and resources to the North. The Union achieved similar success with Generals Jacob D. Cox and William S. Rosecrans pushing former Virginia governor Henry Wise back across the New River by early fall. By the close of 1861, West Virginia, now protected by the Federal army, was on its way to becoming the thirty-fifth state; McClellan had been promoted to major general and was reorganizing the main army in the safe confines of Washington; and Confederate generals P. G. T. Beauregard and Joseph Johnston had advanced their forces close to the Federal capital.

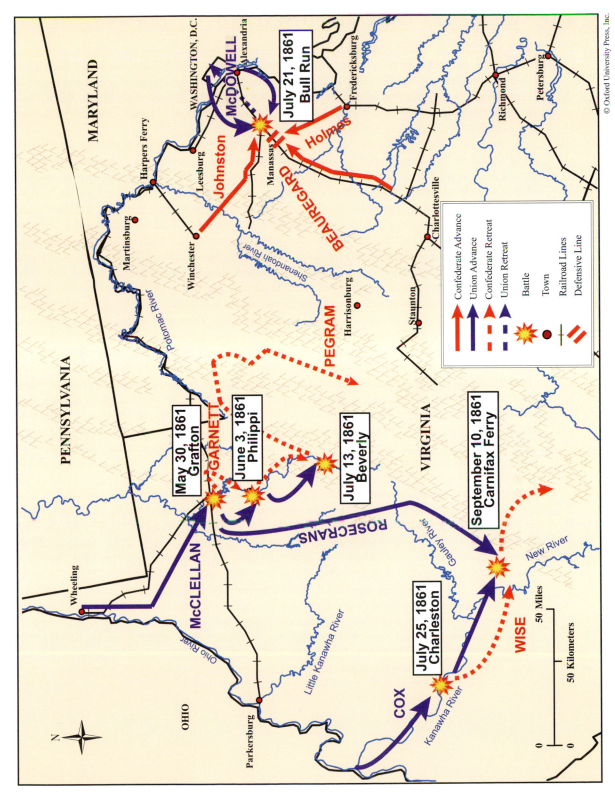

MARYLAND

WASHINGTON, D.C.

Alexandria

McDOWELL

July 21, 1861
Bull Run

Fredericksburg

Petersburg

Richmond

Holmes

Johnston

Harpers Ferry

Leesburg

BEAUREGARD

Manassas

Charlottesville

Martinsburg

Winchester

Shenandoah River

Potomac River

Harrisonburg

Staunton

PEGRAM

PENNSYLVANIA

May 30, 1861
Grafton

GARNETT

June 3, 1861
Philippi

July 13, 1861
Beverly

VIRGINIA

September 10, 1861
Carnifax Ferry

ROSECRANS

Gauley River

New River

Wheeling

McCLELLAN

July 25, 1861
Charleston

WISE

Ohio River

OHIO

Little Kanawha River

Parkersburg

COX

Kanawha River

N

Confederate Advance
Union Advance
Confederate Retreat
Union Retreat
Battle
Town
Railroad Lines
Defensive Line

50 Miles

50 Kilometers

0

0

19

10 WEALTH IN THE UNITED STATES

One of the chief differences between the two sections of the country before the war was their investment strategies. Northerners invested their money in land; bonds; joint-stock companies dedicated to building canals, railroad lines, and industries; and the shipping companies, railroad corporations, and factories that populated the rapidly developing American economy. Southerners invested the majority of their capital in land and slaves. These decisions had enormous consequences for the ability of each side to wage war.

Southern states held much of the national wealth and on a per capita basis white Southerners were wealthier than their peers to the north. This was a result of the vibrancy of the South's slave-based economy within the larger global market. By midcentury, the South was producing some of the most valuable crops in the world. Southerners held a virtual monopoly on cotton production, supplying the imperial engines of Great Britain and France with the fuel they used to establish influence around the world. But in most southern states, a majority of that wealth was fixed in relatively illiquid investments. Slaves continued to be bought and sold during the war, but they could not be converted to gold in order to buy supplies for Confederate armies. The result was a serious lack of accessible capital in the South to fund the war effort. The Confederacy exacerbated this situation with shortsighted monetary policies. Christopher Memminger, the Confederate treasury secretary, preferred a pay-as-you-go approach to the war, a virtual impossibility given the distribution of Southern capital. In each section, the government had three choices for financing the war: taxes, bonds, and printed currency. In each section, the governments pursued a mix of all three approaches, but the Confederacy leaned far too heavily on paper money, with the predictable result of a continually depreciating currency and continually escalating inflation. The Confederacy funded about a third of its war expenses through bonds, almost 60 percent through printed money, and only 8 percent through taxes. The government enacted a wide variety of taxes on income, production, and eventually a "tax-in-kind" on farm goods, which served only to anger Confederate citizens who saw their own government as more fiscally oppressive than the Union government had been before the war. Whereas tax policies inspired animosity, the currency policy only increased hardship, driving up prices for everyday goods and exacerbating the effects of the blockade for everyday consumers.

In contrast, the Union maintained a fairly even balance between the various financing means, raising roughly one-third of the cost of the war with the three methods of taxes, bonds, and paper money. Unlike the Confederate currency, the Union's "greenback" held most of its value over the war. Eventually, the government released $450 million in paper currency, to the dismay of hard-money advocates, and it continued to be used for years after the war. In an innovative move, the Treasury Department gave permission for private financiers, most notably New Yorker Jay Gould, to sell the war bonds. Going door-to-door, the bond salesmen conflated patriotism and profit (the bonds were guaranteed to return a fixed 6 percent) and sold millions. The result was a stable supply of revenue for the Union and a way to ensure that Northerners were literally invested in the war effort. At the same time, Northerners complained, just like Southerners, about new taxes but these fell more lightly on average consumers because the government still drew revenue from excise taxes on imported goods, something the blockade effectively prevented the Confederacy from doing.

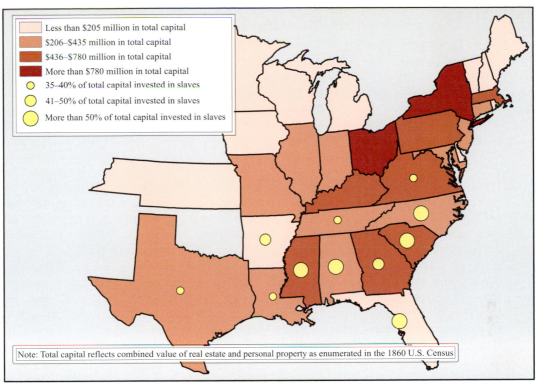

Less than $205 million in total capital

$206–$435 million in total capital

$436–$780 million in total capital

More than $780 million in total capital

○ 35–40% of total capital invested in slaves

○ 41–50% of total capital invested in slaves

○ More than 50% of total capital invested in slaves

Note: Total capital reflects combined value of real estate and personal property as enumerated in the 1860 U.S. Census

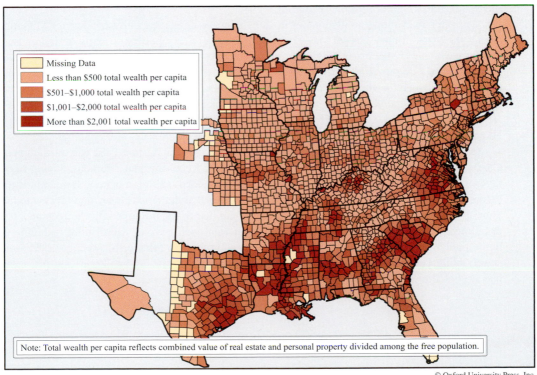

Missing Data

Less than $500 total wealth per capita

$501–$1,000 total wealth per capita

$1,001–$2,000 total wealth per capita

More than $2,001 total wealth per capita

Note: Total wealth per capita reflects combined value of real estate and personal property divided among the free population.

11 MISSOURI

The campaigns in Missouri in the first year of the war reflected the difficulty of securing the loyalty of the border for both North and South. The Union won the contest: by mid-1862, it secured physical control over most of the state, which was retained through the duration of the war. The Union also drew more popular support from Missouri's population, enlisting 45,000 men to the 20,000 who enrolled in Confederate units. Lincoln identified the necessity of retaining the loyalty of the slaveholding border states early in his presidency, and he used his considerable political skills effectively in this region to avoid alienating lukewarm Unionists or empowering eager Confederates. Northern success in Missouri established the pattern that eventually produced a Union victory in the war: control of the rivers and the West, with Federal forces moving steadily south and east.

The fighting in Missouri occurred south of the Missouri River; the half of the state north of the river was controlled by the Union for the duration of the war. The contest began in the spring of 1861, as slaveholding states considered whether or not to organize conventions empowered to discuss and vote on secession. A majority of Missouri's state legislators leaned toward secession, although only a minority of citizens supported such a position. Union general Nathaniel Lyon, recognizing the importance of forestalling action of the state legislature in the wake of the fighting at Fort Sumter, drove the legislature from the capital. Confederates retreated south under the command of Missouri governor Claiborne F. Jackson, where they defeated Lyon's troops at Carthage before moving into northwest Arkansas. Reorganized under the command of Benjamin McCullough, Confederates advanced north and defeated the Federals at Wilson's Creek and then again at Lexington. Despite their victories, Confederates did not have the manpower to secure control of the capital at Springfield. In early March 1862, Union general Samuel Curtis advanced into Arkansas and decisively defeated the Confederates, now under the command of Earl Van Dorn, at Pea Ridge, ending their challenge for control of the region.

The effective Union domination of the state did not ensure a peaceful existence for Missourians during the war. Military control was exercised lightly here, as opposed to parts of Tennessee and Virginia, which were occupied heavily by large armies from both sides. The result was that Missouri was consumed by a guerrilla war that killed thousands of civilians, often in shockingly brutal fashion. Pro-Confederate civilians, known as Bushwackers, and pro-Union civilians, known as Jayhawkers, battled throughout the years of the war and beyond in many places, keeping the population perpetually terrorized. "Bloody" Bill Anderson, William Quantrill, and Frank and Jesse James, for instance, all gained fame as wartime terrorists before they entered American folklore as popular heroes.

A signal event in the battle for control over Missouri came in August 1861 when Union general Charles Fremont issued an order freeing the slaves of all Rebel masters. Fremont, hoping to curry favor with the abolitionists and radical Republicans, expanded on Union general Benjamin Butler's earlier order declaring slaves who escaped to Union lines "contraband of war" and refused to return them to their masters. By declaring free all slaves, not just those employed by Confederates forces or belonging to pro-Confederates, Fremont's order went well beyond what Butler had done. Fremont's order generated acclaim from abolitionists and others in the North and angered Missouri's slaveholding Unionist majority. This was precisely the type of heavy-handed policy that Lincoln had struggled to avoid and he immediately rescinded Fremont's order.

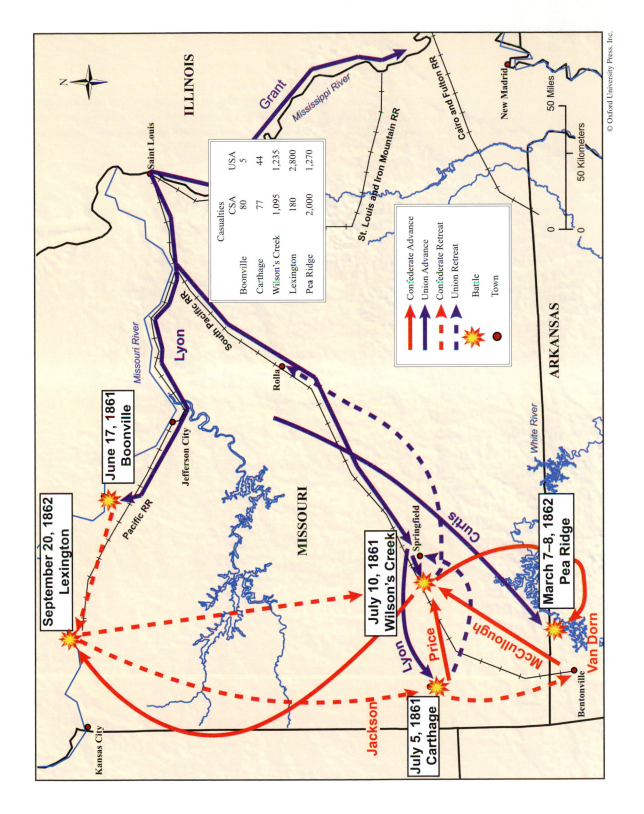

ILLINOIS

Grant

Mississippi River

Saint Louis

St. Louis and Iron Mountain RR

Cairo and Fulton RR

New Madrid

50 Miles

50 Kilometers

Casualties	CSA	USA
Boonville	80	5
Carthage	77	44
Wilson's Creek	1,095	1,235
Lexington	180	2,800
Pea Ridge	2,000	1,270

Confederate Advance
Union Advance
Confederate Retreat
Union Retreat
Battle
Town

Missouri River

Lyon

South Pacific RR

Rolla

June 17, 1861
Boonville

Jefferson City

Pacific RR

September 20, 1862
Lexington

ARKANSAS

White River

MISSOURI

Springfield

Curtis

March 7–8, 1862
Pea Ridge

July 10, 1861
Wilson's Creek

Lyon

Price

McCulllough

Van Dorn

Bentonville

Jackson

July 5, 1861
Carthage

Kansas City

N

© Oxford University Press, Inc.

23

12 ENLISTMENT

By the end of the conflict, the North had enlisted roughly 2.1 million men into its armies. The Confederacy enlisted nearly 1 million. After the war, Lost Cause historians of the event argued that Northern victory was inevitable owing to the population advantage enjoyed by Federals. This might have been true if the North had consistently applied its numerical advantage, but it did not. Instead, the war evolved piecemeal, with Northerners recruiting (often with great difficulty) additional troops as the need became clear. Leading commanders continuously overestimated Confederate troop strength and thus overlooked their own advantages in battle. Most important, the weight given to manpower and material strength overlooks the contingent nature of military events. As Confederate planners knew in 1861, a smartly waged defensive war was more likely to succeed than the North's ambitious plans for conquering a physical space the size of continental Europe.

Although it is true that Northerners had a much wider pool from which to draw when recruiting men, because they waged an offensive war they had a greater need for men. Southerners could, and did, make do with fewer resources. They accomplished this with a more organized and energetic search for volunteers. For both sides, martial enthusiasm and patriotic displays propelled the initial wave of enlistments. After the firing on Fort Sumter, Northern communities sent well beyond the 100,000 men whom Lincoln had called up for ninety-day terms to "suppress the rebellion." Several hundred thousand men came pouring into Washington, D.C., from eastern and western states, deluging the capital and overwhelming the small government's ability to organize them. Troops were barracked in various federal office buildings around Washington, including the Capitol, until more regular facilities could be constructed around the city. Likewise, Southern volunteers flooded Richmond and the country around it in mid-1861, eager for a fight against the Yankees. With perhaps more foresight for an extended struggle, Confederates enlisted for one-year terms, though few in the initial group expected the war to last that long.

Because of the Northern population advantage, they were able to enlist more men but do so with less pressure on individual communities. On average, Northern counties sent 35 percent of their military-age men (defined as 18–35) to fight. In smaller towns, particularly in the Middle West, the tightly knit communities created greater social pressure to join, and percentages ran much higher. Southern counties, in contrast, sent nearly twice as high a proportion of men to fight, roughly 70 percent in many states. Confederates also defined military eligibility differently, beginning with the same 18–35 parameters as the North but concluding with a dragnet that swept in all men ages 17–55. Confederates were also the first to resort to a national draft, an unprecedented event in American history at the time, and one that generated intense opposition within the Confederacy. The Northern government followed a year later with a draft of its own but leaders worked very hard, often through the actions of the Republican Party, to recruit men voluntarily in order to avoid implementing the draft. Enlistment and reenlistment bonuses and furloughs were used by both sides to entice men into the armies. Northern enlistment terms eventually lengthened, as did Southerners', who in 1862 began enrolling men for three years or the war. Both sides also used coercive pressure, shaming men who dodged the draft and increasing penalties for desertion, in order to bolster their number of active soldiers. Reflecting the changing nature of the war in 1863, the North began recruiting African American soldiers, eventually enlisting nearly 200,000. Organized into a separate branch of the service (the U.S. Colored Troops, or U.S.C.T.), these units included former slaves from border and Upper South states as well as free blacks from Northern states.

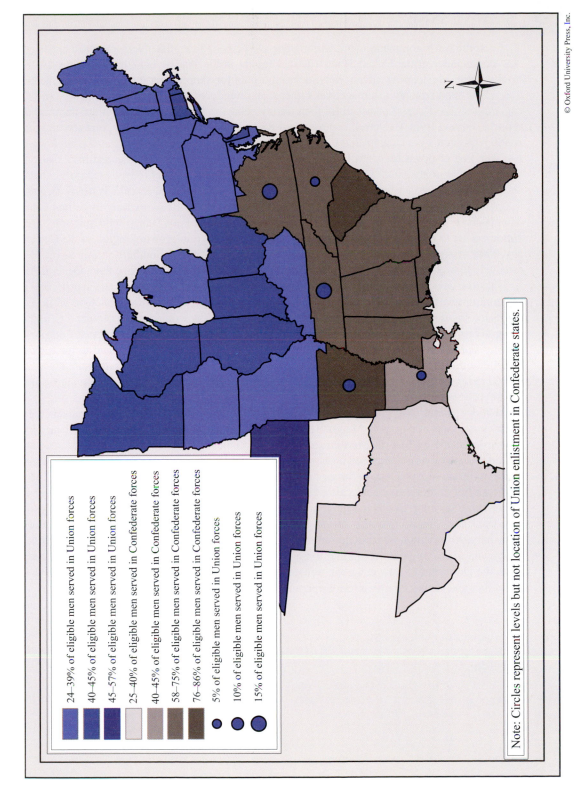

24–39% of eligible men served in Union forces

40–45% of eligible men served in Union forces

45–57% of eligible men served in Union forces

25–40% of eligible men served in Confederate forces

40–45% of eligible men served in Confederate forces

58–75% of eligible men served in Confederate forces

76–86% of eligible men served in Confederate forces

5% of eligible men served in Union forces

10% of eligible men served in Union forces

15% of eligible men served in Union forces

Note: Circles represent levels but not location of Union enlistment in Confederate states.

13 Tennessee

Upon the war's commencement, Union general Winfield Scott, the oldest and most experienced commander in the United States (he had fought in the War of 1812 and directed American troops in the Mexican-American War), devised a plan for suppressing the secession of the South that relied upon strategy and maneuver rather than direct confrontation. With the Northern public eager to see the "Rebels" punished for their unruly behavior, Lincoln pursued a more traditional approach, sending Irvin McDowell south toward Richmond. McDowell's failure, and the underlying wisdom of Scott's plan, compelled Lincoln to adopt its outlines in early 1862.

The first goal was for control of the waterways, and Northern troops launched from Cairo, Illinois, and other points on the Ohio and Upper Mississippi rivers into Confederate territory. The most significant victories came under the leadership of a relative unknown, General Ulysses S. Grant, and Flag Officer Andrew H. Foote, who together succeeded in capturing two vitally important Confederate posts on the Tennessee and Cumberland rivers. Control of Forts Henry and Donelson gave the Union access to two major rivers that led directly into a key grain-growing region of the Confederacy. They also provided access for further advances deeper into the Southern interior. Fort Henry, relatively lightly defended, was captured first and stimulated a quick response from General Albert S. Johnston, who pulled Confederate troops out of Kentucky toward Nashville and sent 15,000 men to shore up the garrison at Fort Donelson. Grant advanced by land toward Donelson while Foote navigated his flotilla up the Cumberland. Confusion within the Confederate command (a continuous problem for Southerners in the Western theater) nullified what had been a successful surprise attack by Confederates on Grant's forces around the fort on February 15. Confined to the fort, with Federal reinforcements arriving, Confederate commanders surrendered to Grant on the 16th. Grant gained fame, stature, and a nickname ("Unconditional Surrender Grant"). The Union gained nearly 14,000 prisoners, strategic positions on both rivers, and open access into Central Tennessee.

Union general John Pope and flag officer Charles H. Davis initiated the Union advance down the Mississippi River in early March. Their first target was the Confederate fort on Island No. 10 and the town of New Madrid, Missouri, just below it on the river. Both positions surrendered and, as at Donelson, Union troops gained both prisoners and strategic advantage. Following the devastating battle at Shiloh in April, Union forces proceeded slowly down the river in early summer. The maneuverability of and heavy guns carried by Union ships enabled them to overcome the defenses at Confederate bastions like Fort Pillow and eventually Memphis. With the capture of Memphis in mid-1862, the Union controlled all of the Mississippi River except the Confederate redoubt at Vicksburg, Mississippi, which required nearly twelve months of siege to capture. Nonetheless, the Union victories along the river in the first half of 1862 proved vitally important. By controlling the river, the Union could slow down the transfer of Confederate troops and material from one theater to another and supply its own interior operations as at Corinth during the battle of Shiloh.

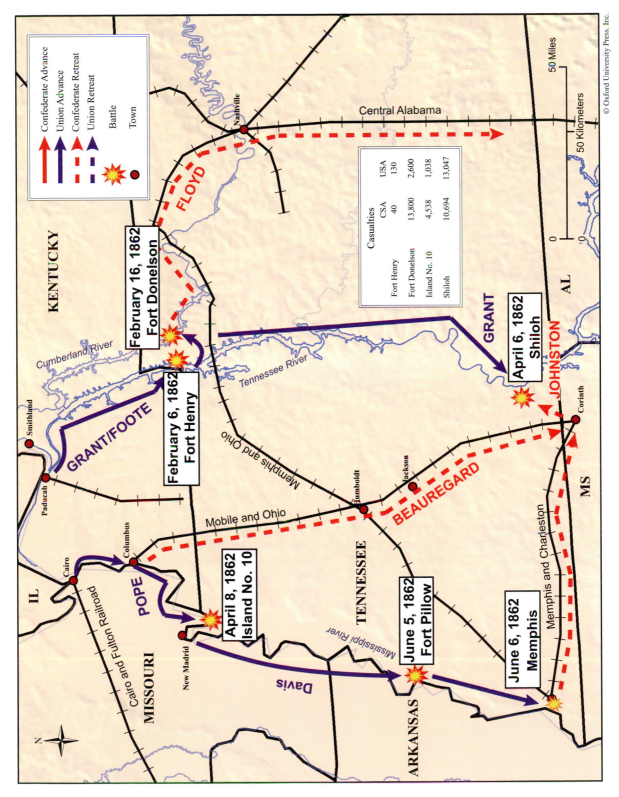

Confederate Advance
Union Advance
Confederate Retreat
Union Retreat
Battle
Town

KENTUCKY

Cumberland River

Smithland

Paducah

IL

Cairo

MISSOURI

Cairo and Fulton Railroad

Columbus

POPE

New Madrid

Davis

April 8, 1862
Island No. 10

Mississippi River

ARKANSAS

June 5, 1862
Fort Pillow

June 6, 1862
Memphis

Memphis and Charleston

Mobile and Ohio

Memphis and Ohio

Humboldt

Jackson

TENNESSEE

BEAUREGARD

Corinth

MS

AL

GRANT

April 6, 1862
Shiloh

JOHNSTON

February 6, 1862
Fort Henry

GRANT/FOOTE

February 16, 1862
Fort Donelson

FLOYD

Nashville

Central Alabama

Tennessee River

50 Miles

50 Kilometers

© Oxford University Press, Inc.

Casualties	CSA	USA
Fort Henry	40	130
Fort Donelson	13,800	2,600
Island No. 10	4,538	1,038
Shiloh	10,694	13,047

N

14 BATTLE OF SHILOH

The first of the monumental battles that came to define the character of Civil War fighting erupted in April 1862 in southeastern Tennessee. The battle, known to Federals as Shiloh for the nearby church and to Confederates as Pittsburg Landing for the section of the Tennessee River along which Northern troops anchored their lines, demonstrated two key elements of the Civil War. For people at the time, Shiloh stood as representative of the nearly unimaginable slaughter that characterized so many later battles; in two days of fighting, Northerners and Southerners inflicted on each other nearly 24,000 casualties. The other significant aspect of the battle, though one that became clear only with time, was the success of Union arms in the West. After the losses earlier in the year at Forts Henry and Donelson and Memphis, all of Tennessee lay exposed to Union control. On the first day of the battle, Confederates came close to destroying the Union army in the region and, if successful, they could have recaptured much of the state. Their failure signaled the permanence of the Federal advance and foreshadowed the westward route that would carry the North to ultimate victory in the war.

The battle itself played out in the disjointed and unpredictable pattern typical of most large-scale Civil War engagements. In early April, A. S. Johnston, the ranking Confederate commander in the west, organized the troops scattered around southwestern Tennessee, northeastern Mississippi, and northwestern Alabama for a surprise attack on Grant's forces stationed at Pittsburg Landing. The surprise worked and on April 6, Johnston's troops stormed into Union camps at dawn. The Confederates successfully pushed back the disorganized Federals and should have won a complete victory, but for stubborn resistance along the Hamburg-Purdy Road at locations—the Shiloh Church, the "Hornet's Nest," Sarah Bell's Peach Orchard—that became synonyms for bloody fighting. According to William T. Sherman, who commanded a Union division, "the scene on this field would have cured anyone of war." Union defenders withstood several hours of attacks, giving Grant enough time to organize defensive lines in front of the river. During the first day of fighting, Johnston was hit in the leg and bled to death before receiving help. His death deprived the Confederacy of their highest-ranking and most experienced general officer.

Thanks to the arrival of Don Carlos Buell's reinforcements during the night, Grant was able to add 20,000 fresh Union troops to the renewed fighting in the morning. Union counterattacks succeeded in pushing the Confederates back, but an able defense, this time organized by General P. G. T. Beauregard, who succeeded Johnston, allowed the Confederates to withdraw in orderly fashion to their stronghold at Corinth, Mississippi. The fighting on both days had been vicious and personal and the battlefield, littered with the detritus of men and equipment, shocked the survivors. Equally appalled were the citizens of each nation who read casualty reports with incredulity. The previous year's battle of Bull Run had been the largest land engagement in North America; Shiloh's casualty count surpassed that one by a factor of almost eight. The decision of people in both regions to continue the war after Shiloh signaled a willingness to accept a high price for ultimate victory in the war. In the near term, the battle's conclusion left Union forces poised to attack Corinth and capture the Memphis & Charleston Railroad, the key east-west route that connected Deep South and seaboard states.

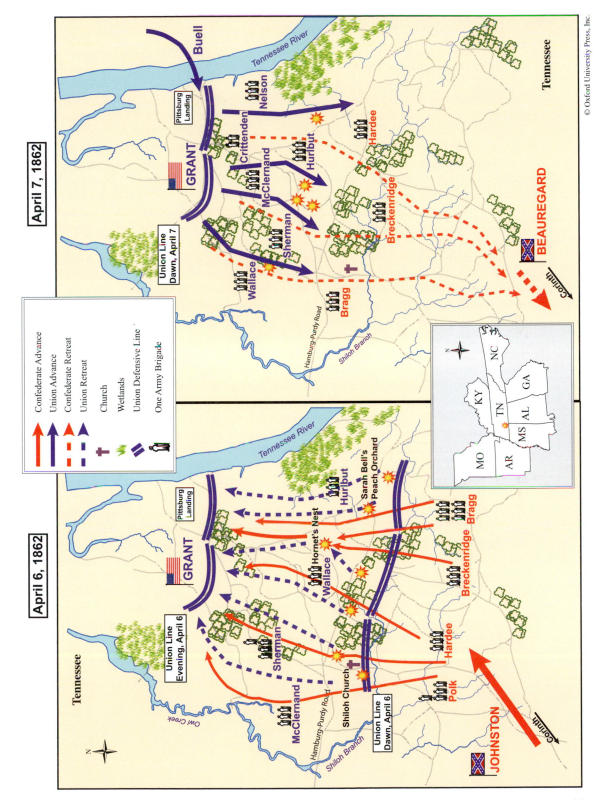

© Oxford University Press, Inc.

April 7, 1862

Tennessee

Tennessee River

Buell

Pittsburg Landing

GRANT

Nelson

Crittenden

Hardee

McClernand

Hurlbut

Breckenridge

Union Line Dawn, April 7

Sherman

Wallace

BEAUREGARD

Bragg

Corinth

Hamburg-Purdy Road

Shiloh Branch

Confederate Advance
Union Advance
Confederate Retreat
Union Retreat

Church
Wetlands
Union Defensive Line
One Army Brigade

April 6, 1862

Tennessee

Tennessee River

Pittsburg Landing

GRANT

Hurlbut

Sarah Bell's Peach Orchard

Bragg

Hornet's Nest

Wallace

Breckenridge

Union Line Evening, April 6

Sherman

Hardee

Owl Creek

McClernand

Hamburg-Purdy Road

Shiloh Church

Polk

Union Line Dawn, April 6

JOHNSTON

Corinth

Shiloh Branch

KY
TN
NC
MO
AR
MS
AL
GA

15 SHENANDOAH VALLEY

The battles of spring 1862 in the Shenandoah Valley involved relatively modest-size armies and small casualty figures, but their significance went well beyond numbers. The principal effects of the Valley campaign were twofold for the Confederates: Stonewall Jackson's victories provided a crucial morale boost for the nation, coming as they did during a period of defeats for the Confederacy. Many citizens saw a national metaphor in the ability of Jackson's smaller but more nimble troops to outmatch the well-supplied and numerous hosts of the Union. In strategic terms, Jackson's victories ensured that tens of thousands of Union troops remained tied up through the spring of 1862 when Union general George McClellan was requesting their help in his campaign against Richmond. Of particular importance in this regard was the necessity of sending General McDowell from Fredericksburg not to reinforce McClellan but into the valley to chase down Jackson. For the Union, the Valley campaign was a humiliating defeat, one that weakened the president and his party politically and signaled the shift of momentum within the war back to the Confederates, on whose side it would remain throughout 1862.

After a cold and disease-ridden winter in camp at Romney, the campaign began inauspiciously with the defeat of Confederate forces at Kernstown. Jackson retreated up and out of the valley but then scored a victory over General Robert Milroy's Union troops at McDowell. After this, Jackson's men continued to see only victories. The defeat of Union garrisons at Front Royal and at Winchester, and the expulsion of Banks from the valley altogether, brought relief and celebration from the Confederate civilians. The Lower Valley remained a dangerous zone of divided loyalties for the rest of the war and Jackson provided only temporary relief from Union occupation, but the 1862 victories provided succor for hard-pressed Confederates in the region for years to come. In late May, Generals Charles Fremont and Irvin McDowell pursued Jackson south but he eluded them yet again. Jackson's success over Fremont at Cross Keys and Port Republic enabled him to move on to Richmond, where he supported Lee in his Seven Days campaign, the opposite of McClellan's intended plan where Union forces would tie up Confederate reinforcements instead.

The tactics and accomplishments of Jackson's army continue to be studied today as an example of how a small force can use the advantages of geography, speed, and deception to immobilize a larger force. He stymied the forces of each of three separate Union commands, led by Banks, Fremont, and McDowell, over the course of four months in early 1862. Jackson's victory depended upon several key factors. A resident of Lexington, in the Upper Valley, Jackson knew the terrain well. He also benefited from the astute geographic intelligence of his mapmaker, Jedidiah Hotchkiss, a Northern-born teacher who was running a school in Staunton when the war broke out. Using Hotchkiss's insights about the landscape of the region, Jackson confused his Union opponents by moving into and out of the valley through the various "gaps" present in the mountains as well as up and down the length of the valley seemingly at will. Jackson's victory also relied on the endurance of his men, who marched over 300 miles in the course of the campaign. The physical toll of this kind of campaigning weakened Jackson's forces even as it bolstered their confidence and generated Union nightmares about elusive and deadly foes.

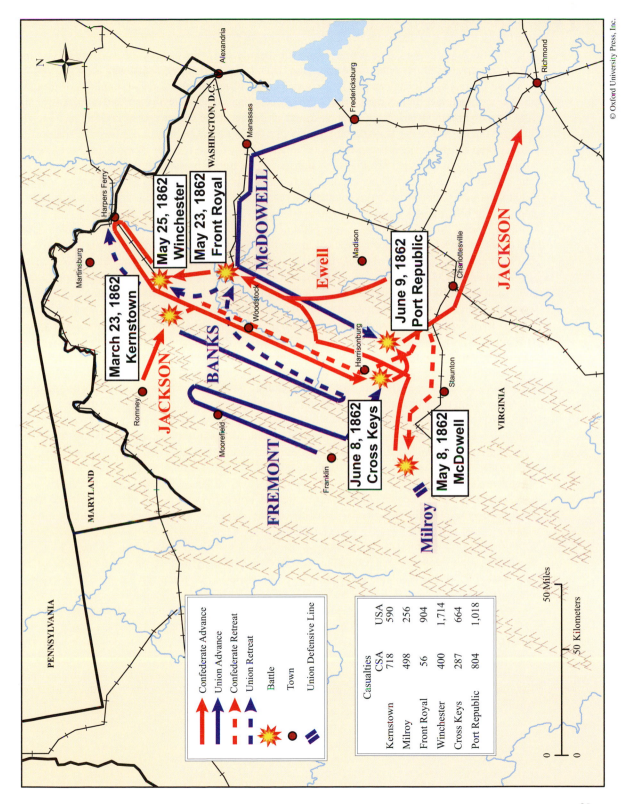

N

© Oxford University Press, Inc.

Alexandria

WASHINGTON, D.C.

Manassas

Fredericksburg

Richmond

Harpers Ferry

McDOWELL

Madison

Charlottesville

Martinsburg

May 25, 1862 Winchester

May 23, 1862 Front Royal

Ewell

June 9, 1862 Port Republic

JACKSON

March 23, 1862 Kernstown

Woodstock

Harrisonburg

BANKS

Romney

JACKSON

Staunton

Moorefield

FREMONT

June 8, 1862 Cross Keys

May 8, 1862 McDowell

VIRGINIA

Franklin

Milroy

MARYLAND

PENNSYLVANIA

	Confederate Advance	Union Advance	Confederate Retreat	Union Retreat	Battle	Town	Union Defensive Line

Casualties	CSA	USA
Kernstown	718	590
Milroy	498	256
Front Royal	56	904
Winchester	400	1,714
Cross Keys	287	664
Port Republic	804	1,018

50 Miles

50 Kilometers

0
0

16 THE PENINSULA CAMPAIGN

After the humiliating Union defeat at Bull Run in July 1861, the main Northern army in Virginia had retreated to the safety of Washington, D.C. Lincoln replaced McDowell with the young, arrogant George B. McClellan. McClellan's specialties were organization and training. All through the late summer, fall, and winter of 1861–1862, McClellan's troops ate, drilled, and prepared for another attempt on the Confederate capital. Union successes in the winter and spring occurred mostly in the Western theater but the Northern public, like the Southern public, understood the real test to lie between the two national capitals. McClellan chose to skip the troublesome land route upon which McDowell had faltered and instead transferred his troops by steamer down the Potomac river and landed them at the tip of the peninsula bordered by the York and James rivers. Fortress Monroe had remained a Union stronghold though the secession crisis and it provided McClellan with a landing spot for his forces.

On April 4, McClellan's troops—numbering over 100,000—began their ponderous advance up the peninsula. McClellan was methodical in the best cases, but during this campaign he relied on faulty intelligence that inflated Confederate defenders by a factor of ten. Thus, John B. Magruder's 10,000 men held McClellan's army at bay before Yorktown for nearly a month, giving Joseph Johnston time to transfer troops to the area. Johnston, a master of the careful defensive retreat, maneuvered his men back toward Richmond as McClellan inched his way forward. Giving up the territory was hard for Virginia soldiers, with one remarking, "We have given up the 'Tide-Water' district; was there ever such a piece of business done in the world?" At the same time, Union gunboats advanced toward the city along the James River. They were eventually stymied by the strong defensive fortifications at Drewry's Bluff, seven miles south of Richmond, a point beyond which they could not pass for the remainder of the war. Although McClellan was a conservative Democrat who marched his troops with clear instructions to respect the property of Southern civilians, the presence of his army inevitably upset the control upon which slavery depended, and thousands of slaves ran to the Union lines seeking their freedom. Unplanned and unmanaged, the collapse of slavery moved in synchrony with the Union advance, just as Southerners had feared it would when they seceded.

When McClellan's troops had reached the outskirts of Richmond—his soldiers could hear church bells tolling alarms to evacuate residents in advance of the imminent capture of the capital—Johnston attacked. The battle at Fair Oaks proved a Confederate defeat and they were forced to retreat once again. But the two positive outcomes of the battle for Confederates were the elevation of Robert E. Lee to command of the army (Johnston was wounded by a shell blast and never regained command) and the temporary immobility of McClellan. Fair Oaks caused more damage than any battle yet on the campaign and McClellan was shocked by the sight of his men wounded and killed. He chose this inopportune moment to reorganize and reoutfit his troops, giving the Confederates a chance to do the same. The sequence of events at this point in the campaign forestalled what looked to most like a foregone conclusion—McClellan's siege and eventual capture of Richmond and with it the end of the war. Had the war ended in early 1862, before Lincoln issued the Emancipation Proclamation, it would have produced a markedly different postwar United States. As it was, McClellan never made his siege. While he prepared his troops for an attack on Richmond, Lee was organizing a counteroffensive that eventually proved successful. The Union advance after the battle of Fair Oaks would be the closest a Northern army would come to the Confederate capital until the spring of 1865.

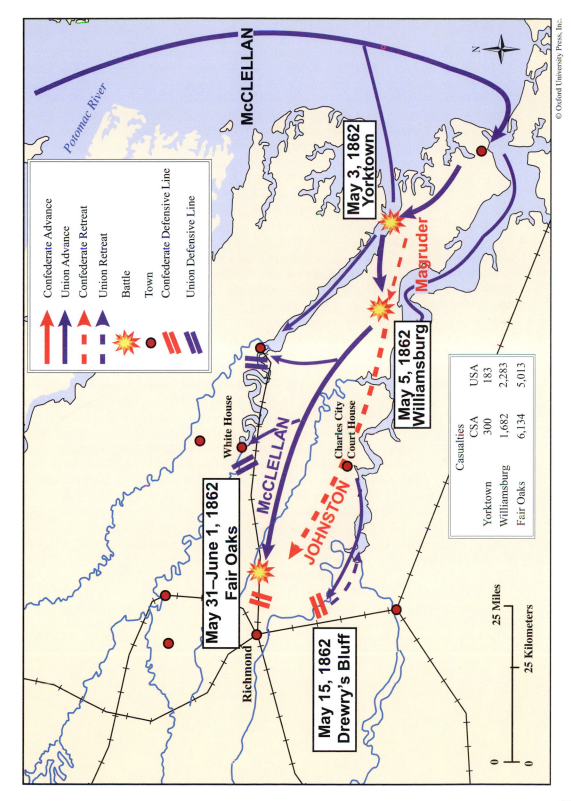

Potomac River

McCLELLAN

N

May 3, 1862
Yorktown

Magruder

Confederate Advance
Union Advance
Confederate Retreat
Union Retreat
Battle
Town
Confederate Defensive Line
Union Defensive Line

May 5, 1862
Williamsburg

White House

Charles City
Court House

McCLELLAN

JOHNSTON

Casualties		
	CSA	USA
Yorktown	300	183
Williamsburg	1,682	2,283
Fair Oaks	6,134	5,013

May 31–June 1, 1862
Fair Oaks

25 Miles

25 Kilometers

Richmond

May 15, 1862
Drewry's Bluff

17 | THE SEVEN DAYS CAMPAIGN

In most cases, an artillery shot that nearly kills the enemy's commanding officer should be counted an asset, but this was not the case for the Union shell that disabled Joseph Johnston. It allowed Robert E. Lee to assume command in Virginia. He initiated an energetic defense of the state that stymied Union troops for three years. Lee's approach often put him in the position of attacking, as he did throughout the Seven Days, but he always kept the fundamentally defensive goals of the Confederacy in mind. Above all, Lee's target was Northern public opinion—if he could make the war too costly or too long, Northerners might withdraw their support for the conflict and give the South its independence. The fighting around Richmond in the seven days at the end of June 1862 cost the Union thousands of lives and derailed soft Northern assumptions about a quick end to the war.

Over the course of the week from June 25–July 1, Lee pushed McClellan's behemoth army back from the outskirts of Richmond to the safety of its gunboats on the James River. He accomplished this with a series of aggressive attacks on the shifting Union position that cost both sides high casualties—20,000 for the Confederates and nearly 16,000 for the Union. Given Lee's recent ascension to command and his relative unfamiliarity with the brigade and division commanders in the army, he succeeded brilliantly where Johnston had failed, but Lee himself hoped for a more definitive destruction of the Northern army. McClellan executed an effective retreat, continually putting his troops in more secure defensive positions, and thus delivered most of them to the secure position along the southern rim of the peninsula.

The campaign opened with a tentative attack by the North on Lee's right flank at Oak Grove. The Confederates halted this drive and initiated their own effort at Mechanicsville, where Lee's troops pushed the Federals out of their defensive lines. The same outcome at Gaine's Mill the following day forced McClellan to pull back over the Chickahominy River. This required that he abandon the formidably supplied base he had established at White House on the Pamunkey River and make a path for Malvern Hill on the James, where Union ships and their heavy artillery lay at anchor. The fighting at Gaine's Mill, as elsewhere throughout the Seven Days, was intense and costly for both sides. From June 28 to July 1, Lee struggled to pin down McClellan's troops. Hindered by McClellan's skill at retreating and the swamps and bogs of the region, Lee inflicted significant damage on Northern forces but could not prevent their escape from the peninsula. Lee's frustration with this outcome showed in his decision to attack the elevated and entrenched Union position at Malvern Hill on July 1. His soldiers marched against Union lines defended not just by ranks of their own cannon but also supported by the large guns on Union warships in the James River. The battle was a wasteful and discouraging failure for the Confederacy and pointed out the long-term vulnerability of the Confederate side: they could not afford to lose four men for every three the Union lost. But in Lee's view, and that of most Confederates, the high cost was offset by the strategic accomplishment of repulsing the Union attack on their capital. Further, Lee followed his victory with a march into the North, putting the Union on the defensive. One of the fundamental questions of the war thus became visible during the Seven Days: Could the Confederacy fight long enough to convince the North to abandon the war?

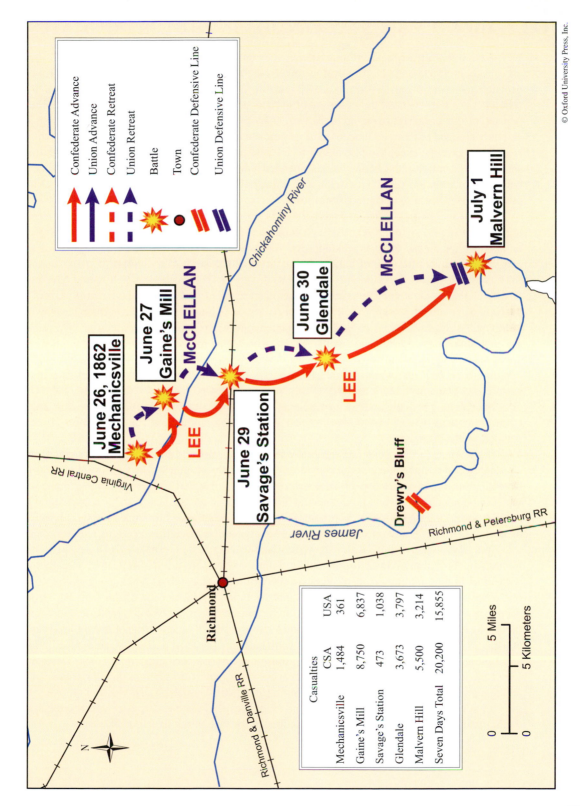

Confederate Advance
Union Advance
Confederate Retreat
Union Retreat
Battle
Town
Confederate Defensive Line
Union Defensive Line

Chickahominy River

July 1
Malvern Hill

McCLELLAN

June 27
Gaine's Mill

McCLELLAN

June 30
Glendale

June 26, 1862
Mechanicsville

LEE

LEE

June 29
Savage's Station

Drewry's Bluff

Virginia Central RR

James River

Richmond & Petersburg RR

Richmond

Richmond & Danville RR

N

Casualties	CSA	USA
Mechanicsville	1,484	361
Gaine's Mill	8,750	6,837
Savage's Station	473	1,038
Glendale	3,673	3,797
Malvern Hill	5,500	3,214
Seven Days Total	20,200	15,855

5 Miles
5 Kilometers
0
0

35

18   HABEAS CORPUS SUSPENSION IN THE UNITED STATES

The Civil War effort imposed unusual demands on the federal government and, under Lincoln's direction, it responded with novel means. By far the most controversial of these was Lincoln's decision to suspend habeas corpus and jail political prisoners indefinitely. Historians and legal scholars have long debated the propriety of his actions, as contemporaries did at the time. The suspension of this basic right granted to all citizens by the Constitution—to be brought before a judge and duly charged or released if accused of a crime—concerned even Lincoln's supporters, who worried that it gave the executive branch unprecedented powers. Lincoln did not disagree with that assessment. Never before had a president suspended habeas corpus, but he was quick to add that never before had the nation been faced with such a dangerous and difficult enemy, one that (as Lincoln saw it), existed within the United States itself.

When Lincoln took office in March 1861, Congress was out of session and was not scheduled to reconvene until late in the year. At the commencement of hostilities on April 12, Lincoln operated on his own, unable to verify or seek approval for his actions with Congress. One of his earliest war acts was to suspend the writ of habeas corpus in parts of eastern Maryland, principally Baltimore. Slavery was legal in Maryland and the state itself very nearly seceded, which would have put the federal capital in the untenable position of being surrounded by Confederate territory. Lincoln imposed martial law on Baltimore following a sharp rise in public conflict after Sumter. He also indefinitely jailed several loud prosecession newspaper editors. His actions infuriated the chief justice of the Supreme Court, Marylander Roger Taney, who sat as the circuit court judge for Baltimore. Taney issued an opinion, *ex parte Merryman*, demanding the release of a jailed editor and condemning Lincoln's suspension of habeas corpus as unconstitutional. Taney argued that only Congress could suspend the writ and that if the order was allowed to stand, "the people of the United States are no longer living under a government of laws." Lincoln ignored Taney's decision and Merryman remained behind bars. Over the next year, Lincoln authorized the suspension of the writ throughout the Northeast.

The Northern response to these events was mixed. Democrats and many conservative Republicans expressed outrage and warned of tyranny; they saw the suspension as unwarranted and illegal. Lincoln himself had been a conservative before the war (and arguably remained one on many issues, including emancipation), and he did not come to the decision to suspend habeas corpus lightly. His explanation rested on his desire to preserve the Union—whether, as he said, he should respect one clause of the Constitution only to see the whole document destroyed—and on his reading of the letter of the law—which specifies that the writ of habeas corpus shall not be suspended "unless when in cases of Rebellion or Invasion the public Safety may require it." Republicans generally agreed with Lincoln that his limited suspensions of the writ were acceptable. When Congress reconvened in the fall of 1861, it voted retroactively to approve Lincoln's suspension of the writ. The strongest support for confirming the decision came from the northernmost band of congressional districts and the strongest opposition from the southernmost band, especially Missouri, southern Illinois and Indiana, and Kentucky. These sections of the North harbored the most people dissatisfied with the war and Lincoln's method of prosecuting it and those most at risk for being imprisoned. Despite their fear, Lincoln did not arbitrarily use this authority—newspapers throughout the war published vituperative and often violent denunciations of him. He did arrest some editors, mostly in regions where the Union exercised only partial control, and he did suspend habeas corpus in specific locales, but the Northern public warily sanctioned his actions in the face of the demands of war.

Note: The legislation was passed in the House of Representatives on December 8, 1862, by a final vote of 90–45.

Legend:
- Approved suspension
- Opposed suspension
- No recorded vote

19 NAVAL CAMPAIGN AND BLOCKADE

The initial Northern strategy contained two strategic elements: to send gunboats down Southern rivers and to blockade the Confederate coastline. The Union only began the former campaign in earnest in early 1862, with the efforts of Foote, Pope, and Grant to secure control of the Mississippi, Cumberland, and Tennessee rivers. The blockade commenced immediately though it failed to take effect for some time. When the war started, the U.S. Navy consisted of fewer than fifty ships, of which over half were at sea and many of the other half in such disrepair as to make them unusable. Confederates could be forgiven for thinking the Northern proclamation to blockade Southern ports was a bit optimistic. In practice, the Union navy consisted of three ships in early 1861. With a 3,000-mile coastline, a number of well-defended deep-water ports, and a long maritime tradition, few Southerners anticipated a serious threat to their economy or territorial integrity from sea. The North faced a legal obstacle as well. Under international law, nations could not blockade their own ports, and because Lincoln insisted that secession was illegal and regarded the seceded states as still in the Union, he seemed to be in an untenable position. Britain became the key arbiter in this dispute—if Britain respected the blockade, it would stand. Although British politicians tended to identify more closely with Southern elites, they foresaw the utility of being able to blockade an unruly imperial port of their own someday and did not make an issue of the contradictions in the Lincoln administration's position. Southerners, for their part, denied the effectiveness of the blockade (also under international law, blockades had to be secure in order to be respected by trading partners) even as they complained about the impropriety of it. In short, the legality and utility of the blockade would be tested in the water.

Under the able leadership of a prewar Democrat, Gideon Welles, the Navy Department moved aggressively forward with the purchase, refitting, and new construction of blockading ships. Welles and his staff worked tirelessly to procure and retrofit merchant ships for use in the navy. They also invested in the development of new technologies like armor plating, revolving guns, and innovative propulsion designs. Their success was visible along the Atlantic and Gulf coasts, where formidable blockading squadrons began to assemble in 1862. The Confederates saved the Union some work by imposing a voluntary boycott on cotton trading with Europe, an attempt to force diplomatic recognition with the power of King Cotton. Nonetheless, the Northern blockade did real damage to the Confederate economy, cutting off not just the lucrative cotton smuggling but also the entry of arms, medicine, and other supplies into the increasingly beleaguered Confederacy. The blockade contributed to the scarcity of goods in the South, which, in turn, exacerbated the rampant inflation in the country.

The blockading squadrons also launched attacks on Confederate ports. The most famous of these clashes was the battle of the ironclads at Hampton Roads, Virginia, in early 1862, where the arrival of the USS *Monitor* forced the Confederates to scuttle the CSS *Virginia* (formerly the USS *Merrimack*) and allowed McClellan's peninsular invasion to take place. Though less dramatic, the steady seizure of Confederate seaports played a key role in the Union war effort. The early loss of Cape Hatteras and Port Royal Sound and the Sea Islands in 1861 gave the North a vital refueling station and a base from which to build the South Atlantic Fleet. The capture of New Orleans in early 1862 brought the South's largest city under Union control for the remainder of the war and made other Gulf Coast ports vulnerable. Though hardly watertight in 1862, the Union blockade became an increasing important part of the Northern war effort.

N

WORDEN

STRINGHAM

DuPONT

Atlantic Blockading Squadron

STEVENS

Atlantic Ocean

300 Miles

300 Kilometers

0

0

© Oxford University Press, Inc.

NEW JERSEY

PENNSYLVANIA

WASHINGTON, D.C.

VIRGINIA

OHIO

KENTUCKY

TENNESSEE

ARKANSAS

MISSISSIPPI

ALABAMA

LOUISIANA

FLORIDA

NORTH CAROLINA

SOUTH CAROLINA

Wilmington

Charleston

Savannah

Mobile

Sabine Pass

Galveston

Key West

FARRAGUT

Gulf Blockading Squadron

March 8–9, 1862
Hampton

August 29, 1861
Hatteras

November 7, 1861
Port Royal

March 12, 1862
Jacksonville

May 10, 1862
Pensacola

April 29, 1862
New Orleans

Union Advance

Confederate Port

Union Port

Battle

Union Blockading Force

39

20 VIRGINIA

After McClellan's defeat before Richmond, Lincoln gave John Pope command of a new Army of Virginia, which he hoped would bring the North a victory in the East. As Lee advanced north from Richmond, Pope ventured out of the safety of fortified Washington with grave pronouncements about the new war against the Rebels. Pope initiated what one historian has aptly termed a "hard war." Though its later practitioners, Grant and Sherman, would perfect the style, Pope gained early infamy in Virginia for his approach. He ordered his army to forage for food when necessary, which many Southerners interpreted as a license to plunder, and declared white men of military age not in the Confederate army eligible for arrest based on the likelihood of their pro-Southern sympathies. Although neither of these orders was enforced with much vigor (very few arrests were made), Pope earned the enmity of Virginians, especially Lee, who savored the opportunity to defeat him.

Pope commanded the collected forces that Jackson had faced earlier in the year in the Shenandoah Valley and awaited reinforcements from McClellan's troops on the peninsula. On the march north, Lee detailed Jackson to the west, where he crossed the Rapidan River and defeated, yet again, Nathaniel Banks and a contingent of Union troops at Cedar Mountain. Pope withdrew toward Manassas to await the arrival of reinforcements, finally released by McClellan, who sent them north by steamer. Lee followed, sending Jackson on a long march to the west. Jackson's troops circled around and surprised Pope's right, capturing the heavily provisioned supply depot at Manassas Junction. After a quick meal of canned smoked oysters, Jackson's troops engaged Pope's on the old Bull Run battlefield. Fighting amid the half-buried corpses and detritus of the previous year's battle lent the scene an eerie otherworldliness, but Jackson's corps held their ground until the arrival of the main force of the army under Lee and his other corps commander, James Longstreet.

From August 28–30, the two sides clashed in ferocious fighting. Pope launched a series of unsuccessful attacks on the entrenched Confederates and the Confederates counterattacked, driving the Federals from the field. The battle ended in a strangely similar fashion to the conclusion of the first battle of Bull Run, with Union troops retreating hastily to the safe confines of Washington, D.C., and Confederates confidently in control of the Virginia battlefield. The defeat further depressed Northern public morale, already weak after McClellan's failure on the peninsula. The bluster with which Pope had left Washington only further embarrassed the army and the nation. The Confederates had also succeeded in inflicting far more casualties than they suffered—losing 9,200 to the Union's 16,000. Nonetheless, Lee's losses since assuming command in June were considerable: at least 31,000 casualties plus significant numbers of deserters and stragglers who fell out during the march north through Virginia. But Lee's strategic success endeared him to his men and enshrined him at the top of the pantheon of Confederate heroes. Most important, the battle signaled the decisive shift of momentum that began with Lee's ascension to command outside Richmond. The pace of the war in the east was now controlled by the Confederates and, much to the consternation of Northerners, Lee's army seemed poised to invade the North and bring the war to their homes.

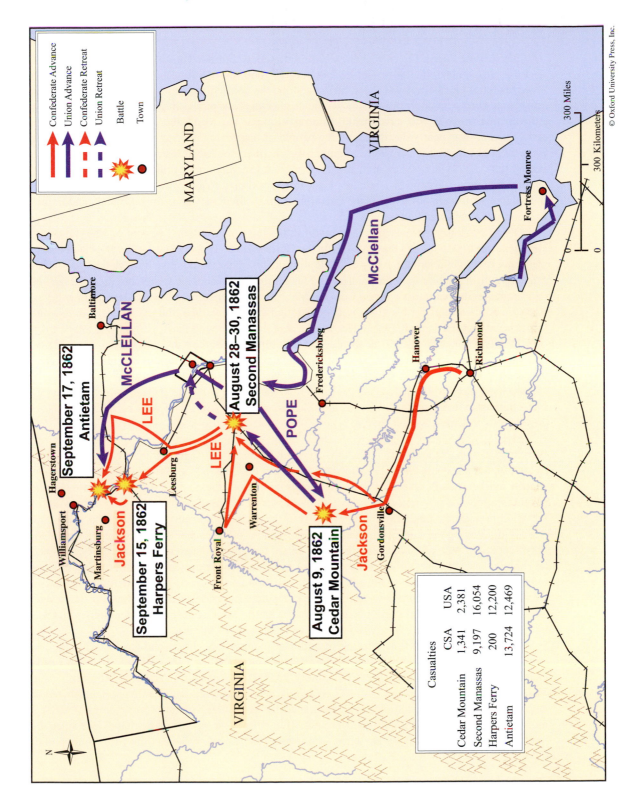

Confederate Advance
Union Advance
Confederate Retreat
Union Retreat
Battle
Town

MARYLAND

VIRGINIA

300 Miles

300 Kilometers

© Oxford University Press, Inc.

Fortress Monroe

McClellan

Baltimore

McClellan

LEE

LEE

LEE

McCLELLAN

September 17, 1862
Antietam

August 28–30, 1862
Second Manassas

POPE

Fredericksburg

Hanover

Richmond

Hagerstown

Williamsport

Martinsburg

Leesburg

Warrenton

Front Royal

Gordonsville

Jackson

Jackson

September 15, 1862
Harpers Ferry

August 9, 1862
Cedar Mountain

VIRGINIA

N

Casualties	CSA	USA
Cedar Mountain	1,341	2,381
Second Manassas	9,197	16,054
Harpers Ferry	200	12,200
Antietam	13,724	12,469

21 BATTLE OF ANTIETAM

After driving Pope's forces back into Washington, Lee continued north. Lee knew that he could not stay long in the North but he had several good reasons for launching the campaign. A close reader of Northern newspapers, he understood the political dynamic at play in the North and knew that even a temporary invasion would further depress public morale and might convince Lincoln that the war was unwinnable. Central Virginia, having hosted two massive armies for nearly a year, was nearly destitute, and the people of that region needed relief from provisioning even their own forces if they were to gather the supplies needed to last the winter. Lee also expected that slaveowning Maryland, still reeling from Lincoln's imposition of martial law, would support his army and send him recruits. Last, Lee hoped that a victory on Northern soil would tip the balance of foreign observers in the direction of the Confederacy and compel Britain and France to recognize the new nation.

Despite serious problems in his army with straggling and desertion, Lee entered Maryland with confidence in his troops and they in him. On the Northern side, Lincoln had sacked Pope and folded the Army of Virginia into the Army of the Potomac, still under the command of McClellan. "Little Mac" remained popular with the soldiers and his return improved their spirits, but the hesitancy he had shown on the peninsula worried Lincoln. McClellan benefited from the accidental discovery of Lee's marching orders for his army, wrapped around three cigars in a Maryland field. Confederate forces were divided and vulnerable. Knowing where they were with the opportunity to attack them individually was a once-in-the-war chance, and unfortunately for the North, McClellan delayed several days before dispatching his army. Lee saw the danger before Northern troops reached him and avoided the catastrophe that could have resulted. McClellan's error gave Jackson's corps time to capture the Union stronghold at Harpers Ferry (and the 12,500 soldiers garrisoned there) and rejoin Lee's defensive line just outside the town of Sharpsburg along Antietam Creek before the main engagement with Union troops.

McClellan intended a simultaneous attack all along Lee's line but owing to unforeseen problems and his own cautious leadership, the battle unfolded in three stages during the day. The Northern failure to coordinate its attacks allowed Lee to shift his limited troops from section to section as needed until Jackson's reinforcements arrived in the late afternoon. The morning fighting in the cornfield along the northern rim of the battlefield was devastating but indecisive. The intensity of the rifle fire leveled a field of ripe corn as neatly as the scythe would have. The same was true of the midday fight along the sunken road, later nicknamed the "bloody lane." Here, Union attacks might have succeeded with reinforcements, but McClellan, fearing a Confederate counterattack, retained an entire corps in reserve throughout the battle. Last, thanks to the presence of a small band of Confederate sharpshooters overlooking the southern section of the creek, Northern forces stalled in front of a low stone bridge nearly all day. Late in the day, Burnside's corps rushed over the bridge, only to be met by A. P. Hill's arriving divisions. The battle was a tactical stalemate, though McClellan claimed victory because Lee was forced to retreat back into Virginia.

Lee's apparent defeat stalled the effort within Britain for recognition and gave Lincoln the impetus to issue the Preliminary Emancipation Proclamation, but the Confederates escaped to fight again. Further, the enormous loss of life—almost 23,000 total casualties in one day's fighting—and McClellan's failure to trap and destroy Lee's army depressed Northern morale and contributed to Republican losses in the fall elections. Infuriated by McClellan's failure to pursue Lee—after a month of waiting, Lincoln finally cabled to ask, "What the horses of your army have done since the battle of Antietam that fatigues anything?"—Lincoln permanently removed him from command of the Army of the Potomac.

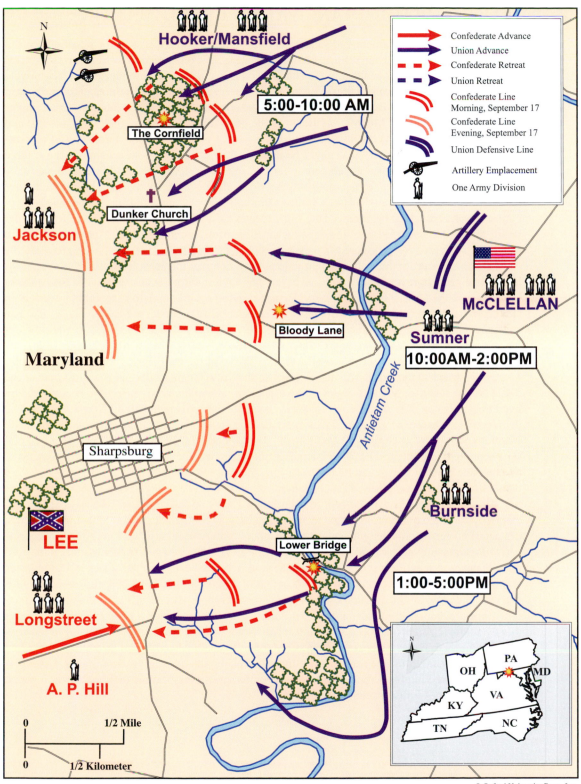

Confederate Advance
Union Advance
Confederate Retreat
Union Retreat
Confederate Line Morning, September 17
Confederate Line Evening, September 17
Union Defensive Line
Artillery Emplacement
One Army Division

Hooker/Mansfield

5:00-10:00 AM

The Cornfield

Dunker Church

Jackson

Maryland

Bloody Lane

McCLELLAN

Sumner

10:00AM-2:00PM

Sharpsburg

Antietam Creek

LEE

Burnside

Lower Bridge

1:00-5:00PM

Longstreet

A. P. Hill

0   1/2 Mile

0   1/2 Kilometer

N

OH   PA
       MD
KY   VA
TN   NC

© Oxford University Press, Inc.

43

At the war's commencement, only a handful of farsighted abolitionists saw the possibility of full emancipation in the United States. Not all the slave states had seceded—Missouri, Kentucky, Maryland, and Delaware remained in the Union—and Lincoln continued to repeat his election-year mantra that he had no power as president to outlaw slavery. Several of his commanders in the field pressed ahead regardless. Benjamin Butler, a political appointee from Massachusetts, set an important precedent at Fortress Monroe, on the tip of the peninsula below Richmond, when he declared three slaves who escaped to his lines "contraband of war." Under the reigning terms of war, combatants could confiscate property that might be used by their enemy for war making. Because these slaves had been requisitioned as laborers to build Confederate fortifications, Butler reasoned they could be used by the Union for the same purpose. When their owners approached the fort, they were turned away. Abolitionists saw this as a limited victory; Butler's "contraband" order continued to recognize slaves as property, but it moved the United States closer to emancipation. Lincoln let the order stand, though he rescinded two broader proclamations from commanders in Missouri and South Carolina that, respectively, declared free the slaves of any Rebel master and all slaves in the region.

Lincoln reserved to himself the right to expand or contract the spirit behind Butler's order. At the same time, congressional Republicans began their own statutory attack on slavery, first outlawing slavery in the District of Columbia (with compensation for masters), then prohibiting slavery in all Federal territory, then moving through two Confiscation Acts, which put Butler's order into law and sanctioned the emancipation of all slaves of Rebel masters. These bold policies could be put into effect only with the cooperation of the army officers and soldiers actually in the South. Although few of these men went to war as dedicated abolitionists, many began to support emancipation as the war lengthened. Some did so because they saw emancipation as a way to punish the South, others saw it simply as a strategic move, and a significant minority may have been moved by real compassion as they encountered runaway slaves pursuing freedom behind Northern lines. The demographic pressure of escaped slaves, who saw the stakes in the war much sooner than many Northern politicians, eventually forced Lincoln's hand. Over the course of the war, some 700,000 slaves, out of a total of 3,500,000, fled bondage for freedom. Lincoln needed some way to manage this massive human change and he began casting about in midsummer 1862 for the terms of what would become the Emancipation Proclamation.

Lincoln's cabinet convinced him to wait until a Union military victory. Five days after Antietam, he issued the momentous announcement, asserting as commander in chief that the policy was "an act of justice, warranted by the constitution, upon military necessity." The Preliminary Emancipation Proclamation gave Confederates until December 31, 1862, to lay down their arms. If they did not, all slaves in rebellious states would be declared free. This exempted all slaves in Union states and in Union-controlled territory, which meant all of Tennessee and West Virginia, as well as the parishes of southwestern Louisiana and Virginia's eastern shore. The legalistic tone and hedged nature of the proclamation offended many abolitionists but most celebrated it nonetheless, recognizing that by adding emancipation as a war aim for the North, Lincoln had irrevocably changed the conflict and the direction of American history. Conservative generals like McClellan and Buell opposed the order, but it stood for the remainder of the war. Finally, the most immediate impact was diplomatic. By connecting the Union directly to the global antislavery cause, the proclamation ended Confederate hopes for European recognition.

Nonslaveholding Union counties

Slaveholding Union counties

Slaveholding Confederate counties exempt from the proclamation

Slaveholding Confederate counties subject to the proclamation

23 KENTUCKY–TENNESSEE

As Lee was planning his counteroffensive into occupied Maryland, the Confederacy's main western commander, Braxton Bragg, was plotting a similar strategy for Kentucky. Bragg intended to draw Union forces, under the command of Don Carlos Buell, out of southern Tennessee, rally Kentuckians to the Confederate cause, and shift the initiative to Confederate hands. Although Bragg did bring the war into northern Kentucky, he was repulsed like Lee, and Kentucky remained securely in Union hands for the remainder of the war.

Confederate General Kirby Smith began the campaign, driving out a small Union garrison at Cumberland Gap and proceeding north toward Richmond. The main body of Confederates under Bragg advanced as far as Frankfort, where they installed a pro-Confederate government and held an inauguration for the new governor. One of Bragg's first acts after welcoming the state to the Confederacy was to implement the Draft Act, passed in April 1862. Reasoning that loyal Kentuckians had been unable to enlist because the state remained in the Union, Bragg expected thousands of new recruits. Like Lee in Maryland, however, Bragg received only a lukewarm reception. Those men eager to serve the Confederacy had already enlisted, many crossing the border to join Tennessee units. The result was that many of the men remaining were either loyal to the Union or unfit for service. Most residents bitterly resented the heavy-handed threat of conscription and Bragg accomplished little in the way of winning over the state.

By early fall, Buell headed north in pursuit of Bragg. The two armies collided at Perryville for what would be the decisive battle of the war in Kentucky. Bragg's forces were divided and Buell, who could not hear the battle for most of the day, engaged only nine of his twenty-four brigades, but the battle was hotly contested. Although the Confederates succeeded in pushing the Union line back, Bragg, recognizing he was outnumbered, withdrew. Joined by Smith, Confederate forces abdicated Kentucky and retreated all the way back through Tennessee into northern Alabama. Buell failed to follow, as McClellan had failed to pursue Lee, and he too was relieved of duty, replaced by Williams S. Rosecrans, who would become the highest-ranking Catholic officer in the war. Antietam and Perryville stood as last invasions launched by the Confederacy in 1862.

At the same time that Bragg occupied Federal forces in Kentucky, Confederate generals Sterling Price and Earl Van Dorn engaged Union troops in northeastern Mississippi for control of the vital rail junction at Corinth. In mid-September, Price advanced upon and briefly occupied Iuka but retreated as more Union troops reinforced Rosecrans, then commanding Union forces in the area. Rosecrans stabilized the defenses at Corinth with his 23,000 men and met the attacks of Van Dorn and Price's combined forces on October 3–4. The fighting was brutal but ultimately inconclusive. Despite bloody frontal assaults on Corinth, Confederates could not break the Union position and they were forced to retreat back into Mississippi. The fighting at Iuka and Corinth were the last Confederate offensives in northern Mississippi and their failure ensured that the Union would control the key east-west rail line for the remainder of the war. The actions of Rosecrans's army had been directed by Ulysses S. Grant, ranking commander in the Western theater. Continued Union successes under his direction boosted his reputation and brought him to the attention of Lincoln, who recognized Grant as one of the few commanders who fought and won for the Union.

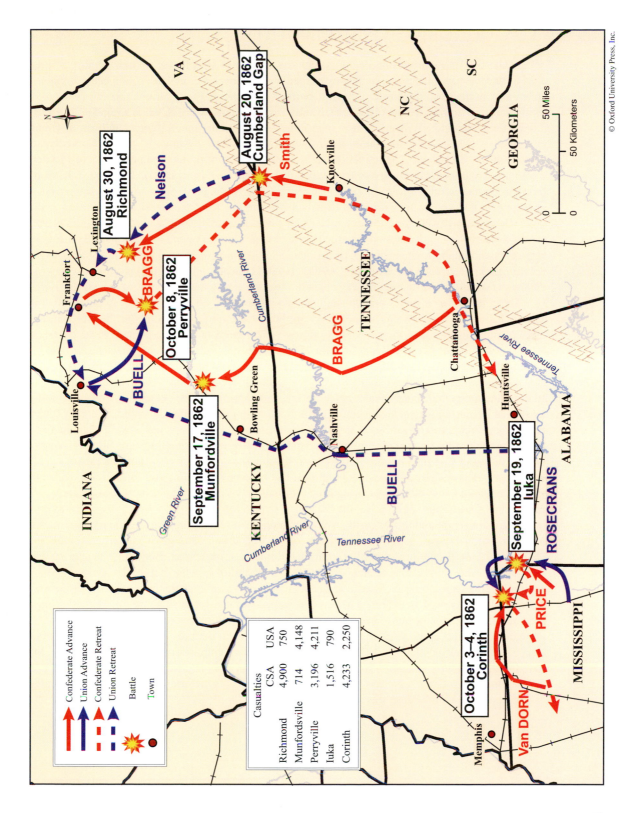

August 20, 1862
Cumberland Gap

August 30, 1862
Richmond

Nelson

Smith

Knoxville

VA

NC

SC

GEORGIA

50 Miles

50 Kilometers

0

0

BRAGG

Lexington

Frankfort

October 8, 1862
Perryville

BUELL

BRAGG

Cumberland River

TENNESSEE

Chattanooga

Tennessee River

Louisville

September 17, 1862
Munfordville

Bowling Green

Huntsville

ALABAMA

INDIANA

Green River

Nashville

BUELL

September 19, 1862
Iuka

KENTUCKY

Cumberland River

Tennessee River

ROSECRANS

PRICE

October 3–4, 1862
Corinth

Van DORN

MISSISSIPPI

Memphis

N

Confederate Advance
Union Advance
Confederate Retreat
Union Retreat
Battle
Town

Casualties	CSA	USA
Richmond	4,900	750
Munfordville	714	4,148
Perryville	3,196	4,211
Iuka	1,516	790
Corinth	4,233	2,250

24 U.S. CONGRESSIONAL ELECTIONS

Despite the year's promising opening, with the capture of Port Royal Sound, South Carolina, Forts Henry and Donelson in Tennessee, and New Orleans in April, the Union cause remained stalemated in the East, the theater upon which most domestic and international observers focused. Particularly frustrating to Lincoln was the Confederates' repulse of McClellan's ponderous efforts to capture Richmond. By late summer, John Pope had joined the ignominious pantheon of Union commanders unable to secure victory in Virginia. Robert E. Lee, meanwhile, led his Confederates northward into Maryland. The retreat of Lee's army at Antietam brought some relief, but McClellan's failure to pursue him frustrated the nation and Lincoln. Like Lincoln, Lee recognized that warfare was, in the words of a leading theorist of the time, "politics by other means." Among other goals, Lee's invasion of the North was planned with the intent of weakening Republicans at the polls. He chose an auspicious time for such a campaign. Regardless of political orientation, Northerners were expressing frustration over the failure of Union arms. Among Democrats and other conservatives, indignation remained high over Lincoln's imposition of martial law and the increasingly harsh Northern approach to war. Abolitionists and other radicals condemned Lincoln's slow pace on emancipation and unwillingness to wage a harder war to destroy the Southern slaveocracy.

The culmination of Lee's invasion and the lack of progress on other military fronts resulted in serious losses for congressional Republicans in the fall elections. Democrats in the North recaptured twenty-eight seats in the new 38th Congress. These gains included a number of state delegations that had been majority Republican in 1860, which now became Democratic majorities, including Lincoln's own state of Illinois. The geographic distribution of the anti-Lincoln vote is striking. The Democrats drew strength from the southern tiers of many northern states, including Illinois, Indiana, Ohio, Pennsylvania, New Jersey, and New York. The center of Democratic resistance was Kentucky, which demonstrated the difficulty presented by the slaveholding border states. Republicans held onto or won seats in the northern tier of those same states as well as maintained their dominance throughout New England and the Upper Midwest. In the final tally, Republicans retained control of Congress but they did so under much more competitive circumstances.

Most observers agreed that Lincoln himself had become a lightning rod for criticism and congressional candidates suffered because of their affiliation with him. Although off-year elections are usually bad for the sitting executive, the breadth of opposition to Lincoln was striking. He was criticized from the right and the left, with even many congressional Republicans unhappy with his administration of the war. Analyzing conditions of the war in late 1862 gives modern observers the chance to see how contingent and uncertain the ultimate outcome was. Both sides began the war with righteousness in their cause and confidence in their ability to achieve it. After nearly two years of fighting, the Union was no closer to achieving its goal of reunion while the seceded states seemed permanently ensconced in their new nation. Two aspects of the war gave pause to those who imagined an imminent conclusion. The Emancipation Proclamation promised a long and hard war. Although it may have contributed to the Democratic victories in the fall, it ultimately gave Republicans another inspiring element with which to rouse Northern enthusiasm for war. In the future, the twin themes of liberty and union would be sounded at every rally and parade. The other ray of hope for the Union was Grant's success in the Western theater. If his victories could be replicated in the east, perhaps the Union cause was not lost after all.

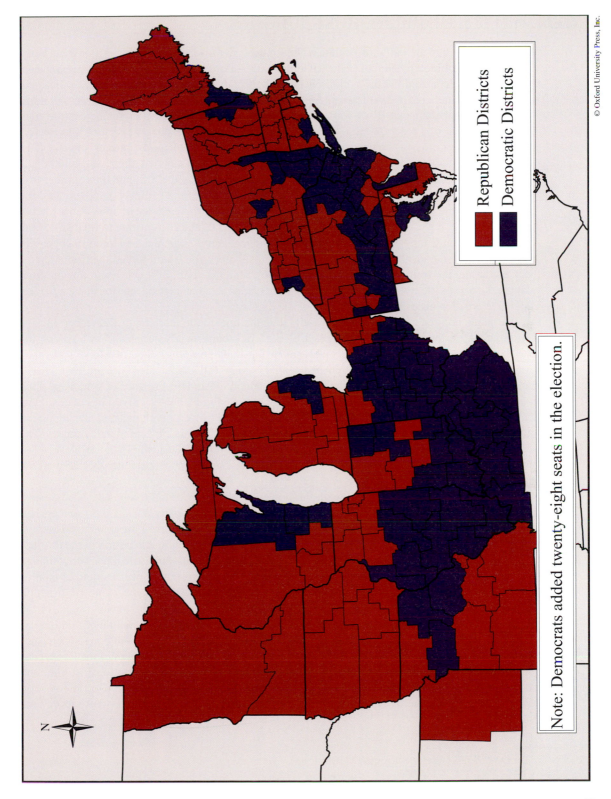

Republican Districts

Democratic Districts

Note: Democrats added twenty-eight seats in the election.

© Oxford University Press, Inc.

49

25 BATTLE OF FREDERICKSBURG

Immediately after the battle of Antietam, Lee moved his troops back over the Potomac River into Virginia. Lincoln had replaced McClellan with Ambrose Burnside, a corps commander in the army who demurred the promotion because he did not feel up to the task. Lincoln insisted, and the army lumbered forward across Virginia toward Richmond. Burnside reached the north bank of the Rappahannock River while Lee followed and occupied the heights across the river behind the town of Fredericksburg. Burnside was impatient to push forward, but high waters impeded the river crossing. When Union engineers finally arrived to build pontoon bridges, Confederate sharpshooters positioned in Fredericksburg buildings harassed them and stalled the work. Burnside issued a warning that he intended to shell the city if the firing on the engineers did not stop. The city had a prewar population of 6,000, and most of the panicked residents fled the city south into the cold wilderness of Spotsylvania County. At the announced hour, Burnside began shelling the town. The destruction caused by this attack, and the ensuing vandalism of the town after Union troops entered its borders, became legendary examples of Union misbehavior within the Confederacy. Bolstered by their own sharpshooters, the Union forced the Confederates back to the defensive line established along Marye's Heights south of town. From this elevated plateau, Lee had a clear view of Burnside's approach and the advantage of interior lines, a perfect defensive position according to the tactics of the day.

Burnside ordered a coordinated attack all along the line on the morning of December 13. The Union attack on the Confederate right, east of Fredericksburg, nearly succeeded in breaking the line, but the main thrust of Burnside's plan called for a charge up the slope of Marye's Heights. Confederates at the top were well entrenched behind a stone wall and fortified with artillery. The attackers were supposed to fan out but the murderous cannon fire and the presence of a drainage ditch funneled the men into a narrow channel. Regiments advanced individually, only to be cut down virtually in their entirety. Wave after wave of blue suits marched forward, eventually advancing on top of the bodies of fallen comrades. None made it even to the first ranks of Confederate infantry. The scale of slaughter prompted Lee's enigmatic comment that "it is well that war is so terrible, else we should grow too fond of it." Burnside, at the pleading of his corps commanders, finally called off the attack late in the afternoon.

Confederates, though impressed with the bravery with which Union troops advanced against the odds, relished the chance for what they saw as well-deserved revenge. When Union soldiers had finally crossed the river and entered Fredericksburg, they broke into many of the abandoned houses, pulling wardrobes into the streets and donning southern finery in a mock celebration of the destruction of the town. Pianos, cutlery, heirloom chests, and assorted household valuables were emptied into the streets and destroyed as Union soldiers unleashed their frustration over battlefield failures in Virginia and the snipers who preyed on their engineers. For Confederates, the wanton destruction of Fredericksburg and the expulsion of its citizens became a symbol of the rapaciousness of the Northern war machine. The cult of national sacrifice reached an apogee in the plight of families exiled into winter forests. Confederates from around the South said prayers and sent donations to support the exiles. The battle itself left Confederates in firm control of Virginia south of the Rappahannock, the Union high command in disarray as Burnside's lieutenants spoke out against him, and desertion skyrocketing among the Federal troops. The humiliating defeat capped a terrible year on the battlefield for the North and demonstrated that reunion would come only after much more time and bloodshed.

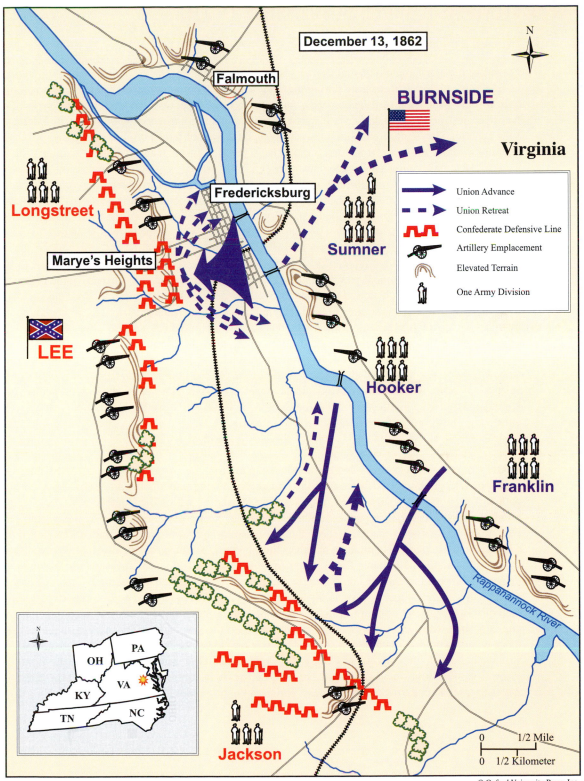

December 13, 1862

Falmouth

BURNSIDE

Virginia

Fredericksburg

Longstreet

Marye's Heights

Sumner

LEE

Hooker

Franklin

Rappanannock River

Union Advance
Union Retreat
Confederate Defensive Line
Artillery Emplacement
Elevated Terrain
One Army Division

Jackson

OH
PA
KY
VA
TN
NC

0   1/2 Mile
0   1/2 Kilometer

© Oxford University Press, Inc.

Just like the North, the South had its own contentious debate over the proper balance of individual freedom and domestic security during the war. Although Southerners were keen to criticize Lincoln for his suspension of habeas corpus, some citing it retrospectively as evidence that secession had been justified, Jefferson Davis inspired nearly as much controversy within the Confederacy. Like Lincoln, Davis imposed martial law, suspended the writ of habeas corpus, and jailed political enemies without trial. These actions, which Davis justified in language strikingly similar to that used by Lincoln, compelled Confederates to weigh the costs of waging war against the potential harm done by staying in or returning to the Union. Davis's most vituperative critics, who included his vice president, Alexander Stephens, and several high-ranking congressional leaders, came close to suggesting that his actions repudiated the very reason for the creation of the Confederacy in the first place. Discussing the president's suspension of habeas corpus, Stephens predicted that "constitutional government will go down, never to rise again on this continent."

The debate within the Confederacy pitted those who advocated the protection of individual liberties at all costs against those who accepted temporary restrictions on civil liberties in the interests of winning the war. One historian has characterized the debate as one between libertarians and nationalists. Stephens, Texas senator Louis T. Wigfall, and Georgia senator Howell Cobb were among the most outspoken libertarians. They argued that suspension of habeas corpus, as well as laws such as the draft, impressment, and the tax-in-kind, represented the kind of political oppression that Southerners had left the Union to avoid. The nationalists, represented by Davis and, most important, Robert E. Lee, responded that although the curtailment of civil liberties was regrettable, temporary suspensions were necessary if the Confederacy were to survive. The presence of strong pockets of Unionism within the South ensured that the Confederacy had active political, and often military, enemies within its borders through the duration of the war.

Whereas Lincoln's first suspension of habeas corpus came before the U.S Congress was in session, Jefferson Davis, perhaps watching the trouble that caused for Lincoln, always requested authority from the C.S. Congress first before imposing martial law. In each of the cases, the Congress held long and often angry debates over the matter. The voting patterns in early 1864 reflected the nature of support for this one aspect of centralizing legislation within the Confederacy. The distribution of support and opposition within the Confederacy was not as clear cut as it was within the Union on similar issues, partly because the Confederacy outlawed party identifications and thus could not impose party discipline on members during votes. Nonetheless, the distribution reveals an interesting geographic feature. Those places that had experienced Union invasion and occupation tended to support the suspension. Northern Virginia, southern Louisiana, southern Kentucky, and many of the congressional districts in the Lower Mississippi Valley showed broad support. Many inland districts, especially South Carolina, Arkansas, and parts of inland North Carolina, rejected arguments about the necessity of martial law and opposed the suspension. This pattern suggests that those people who directly experienced the hard war waged by the North were willing to accept restrictive policies in the interests of victory. The debate over these issues did not destroy the Confederacy as some scholars have suggested, but it created grave tensions and demonstrated how difficult it was to wage a modern war based at least partly on the principles of state rights.

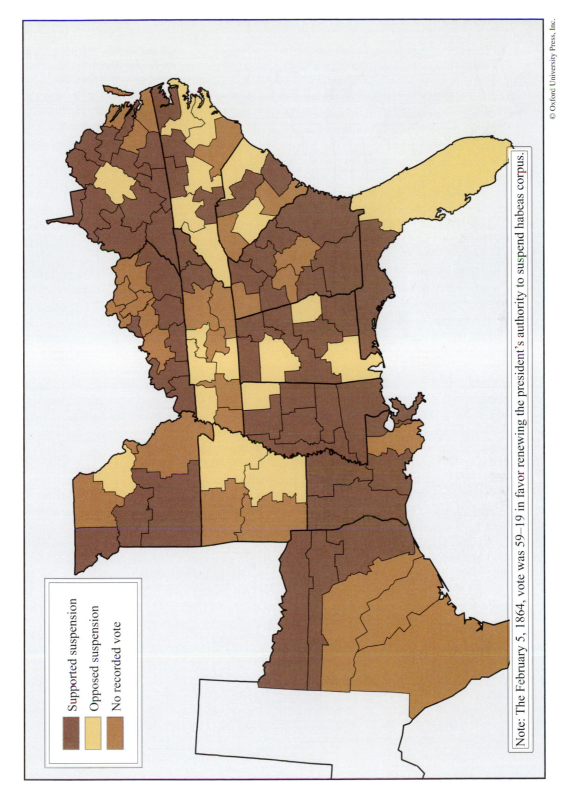

Supported suspension
Opposed suspension
No recorded vote

Note: The February 5, 1864, vote was 59–19 in favor renewing the president's authority to suspend habeas corpus.

27 BATTLE OF CHANCELLORSVILLE

Alongside Stonewall Jackson's 1862 Valley campaign, Lee's generalship in the battle of Chancellorsville is probably the most widely studied and admired tactical action of the war. Lee was aided in this situation by the timid Union leadership opposing him, but the gamble he took, splitting his army not once but twice, demonstrates the deep faith he had in his soldiers to perform almost any task he requested.

After the battle of Fredericksburg in December 1862, Lee's soldiers remained encamped above the Rappahannock River through the winter. The conditions were harsh as the men were generally short of rations and trying also to ensure the survival of the town's residents who relied on charity to sustain themselves. Union troops, on the north side of the river, were better supplied but still experienced a bad season. Morale plummeted after the battle. Evidence from diaries and official reports indicates a sharp rise in desertion, with perhaps 100 men leaving per day in January. In a highly unusual move, several of Burnside's division commanders spoke out against him to War Department officials. With little choice, Lincoln changed commanders again, this time elevating Joseph Hooker to command of the Union's Army of the Potomac. Like McClellan, Hooker was an excellent organizer and he spent much of the spring reequipping and reenergizing the dispirited troops. Like Pope, he was boastful, and he left Washington with confidence and vigor, anticipating a quick end to Lee's army and the rebellion.

Rather than another frontal attack on Lee's entrenched position above Fredericksburg, Hooker detached part of his huge army and marched them west before crossing the river just east of where the Rapidan joins the Rappahannock. Hooker's movement was made with surprising stealth and his troops were across the river before Lee was aware of his departure. Once aware, Lee responded with his usual alacrity. He split the army and left a portion of it at Fredericksburg under the command of another Virginian, Jubal Early. Lee and Jackson proceeded west to meet Hooker, and Lee split the army again, this time sending Jackson's wing far to the west to Hooker's far right side. They surprised a novice corps under the command of Oliver O. Howard and rolled up the Union line. Hooker, surprised to find Confederates on his right and in front, faltered and began to withdraw toward the river. Several days of hard fighting comprise the battle of Chancellorsville, but it was Lee's maneuvering and success that define the engagement. For Confederates, the only bad news in the fight was the accidental wounding of Stonewall Jackson by his own men as he returned from scouting the Union line late at night. Jackson contracted postoperative pneumonia from the wound and died ten days later, depriving Lee and the army of his valuable leadership.

By May 6, Hooker had retreated over the river and was pulling his army back toward Washington. The North looked on in amazement, watching yet another Union commander unable to wrest victory from Lee and his Confederates. The defeat propelled the peace movement to new prominence in the North and inspired more criticism of Lincoln and his military advisors. The battle emboldened the Confederacy and Lee, who once more used a battlefield victory in Virginia to initiate a campaign into the north, this one through Maryland and into Pennsylvania.

Legend
- Confederate Advance
- Union Advance
- Union Retreat
- Confederate Line
- Union Line
- Forested area
- One Army Division
- Church

Falmouth

Fredericksburg

Early

May 3, 1862

Sedgwick

Rappahannock River

Salem Church

Scott's Ford

May 4, 1862

May 6, 1862

April 26–30, 1862

HOOKER

U.S. Ford

Couch

Slocum

Banks' Ford

McLaws

Jackson

April 30–May 1, 1862

LEE

Meade

Sickles

Richards Ford

Howard

Ely's Ford

May 2, 1862

Jackson

Stuart

May 3, 1862

Virginia

3 Miles

3 Kilometers

PA

OH

VA

NC

KY

TN

© Oxford University Press, Inc.

28 THE PENNSYLVANIA CAMPAIGN

In the weeks after the victory at Chancellorsville, Lee sought to transform the army's accomplishment into another invasion of the North. Again, Lee turned to the offensive with an explicitly political intention—if he could capture a Northern city, perhaps Harrisburg, Pennsylvania, even temporarily, it might convince Northerners of the futility of the further fighting. As in the 1862 invasion of Maryland, Lee also sought to relieve logistical pressure on Virginia. During the march, Lee intended to use the Shenandoah Valley to screen the movements of his army, but a U.S. cavalry reconnaissance over the Rappahannock met Lee's cavalry commander, J. E. B. Stuart. The resulting battle at Brandy Station, the largest cavalry battle of the war, was itself inconclusive but it alerted Northern commanders to the fact that Lee's army was on the move.

By mid-June, Richard Ewell's wing of Lee's army attacked and defeated the Union garrison at Winchester, which had been reoccupied by Northern forces after Jackson's exit from the valley in 1862. Winchester may hold the record for the number of shifts in occupation during the war, counted at more than sixty by local historians, and for residents the result was a life of continual uncertainty and danger. Beyond Winchester, Ewell rejoined Lee's army as they crossed through Maryland into Pennsylvania. At the same time, Stuart led the Confederate cavalry east of the Union forces and north into Maryland. Stuart's route was a circuitous one and he remained cut off from Lee for two crucial weeks in late June. With the advent of the rifled musket, which increased the killing range and accuracy of most infantrymen, the cavalry on both sides performed the crucial work of gathering intelligence. With Stuart inaccessible, Lee proceeded blind into Pennsylvania, and, consequently, encountered Union forces where he was not expecting them.

On the march, Lee instructed his troops to treat Pennsylvania citizens with respect, in an attempt to distinguish the upstanding Confederate way of war from the barbarous treatment Fredericksburg residents received at the hands of Yankees. Although Confederates committed few acts of wanton violence, they confiscated property as needed (obligated by Lee's order to compensate civilians, soldiers left Confederate scrip, which was worthless in the North). The Confederate army also seized African Americans during the campaign and sent them back to Virginia. Some of these people may have been runaway slaves from Virginia but others were free men and women living in the North. In either case, the action was a stunning effort by Confederates to repudiate the terms of Lincoln's Emancipation Proclamation. For Confederate soldiers, the campaign into Pennsylvania was the first chance to see the Northern home front during the war and many were dismayed with the apparent prosperity of the rich agricultural land. Confederates marched through the southern Pennsylvania towns of Chambersburg and Carlisle, alarming residents and scaring the North, which had been reared on stories of the ferocity of Lee's fighters.

Although Hooker led his troops north after Lee, his failure at Chancellorsville convinced Lincoln that he was not fit for high command. On June 28, just days before what would be the climactic battle of the campaign, Lincoln replaced Hooker with George G. Meade, a promotion that finally worked. Meade himself was hesitant to accept the command in the middle of a campaign, but he led the Union to victory at Gettysburg and remained in tactical command of the Army of the Potomac for the remainder of the war. Meade understood the importance of repulsing Lee's invasion. After Chancellorsville, Northern public opinion had soured still more on the war and loud voices within the Democratic Party and some outside it were calling for a negotiated end to the apparently hopeless contest. The battle in Pennsylvania would be a critical moment to stall the burgeoning peace movement in the North.

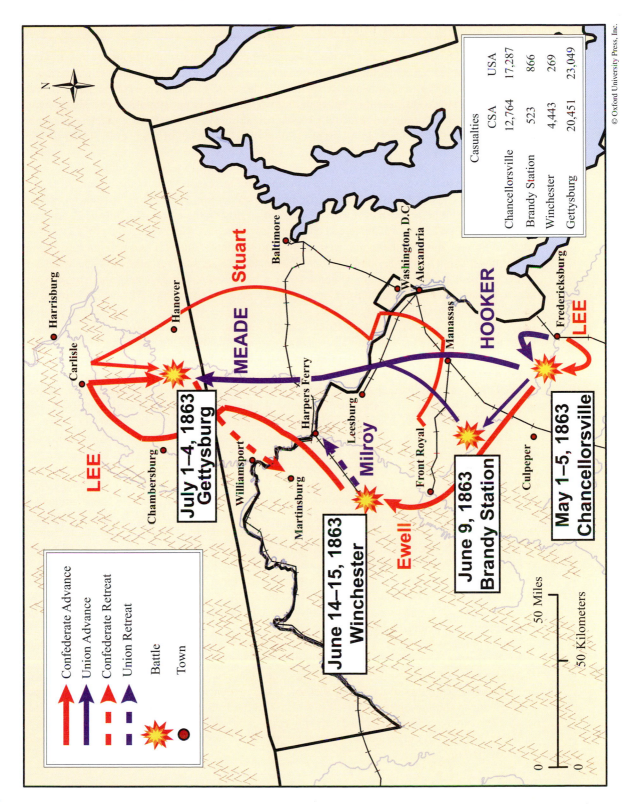

Casualties	CSA	USA
Chancellorsville	12,764	17,287
Brandy Station	523	866
Winchester	4,443	269
Gettysburg	20,451	23,049

Stuart

MEADE

HOOKER

Baltimore

Washington, D.C.

Alexandria

Manassas

Fredericksburg

LEE

Harrisburg

Hanover

Carlisle

LEE

Harpers Ferry

Leesburg

Front Royal

Culpeper

Chambersburg

Williamsport

Martinsburg

Milroy

Ewell

July 1–4, 1863
Gettysburg

June 14–15, 1863
Winchester

June 9, 1863
Brandy Station

May 1–5, 1863
Chancellorsville

N

Confederate Advance
Union Advance
Confederate Retreat
Union Retreat
Battle
Town

50 Miles

50 Kilometers

0

0

29 BATTLE OF GETTYSBURG

Gettysburg stands today as an iconic American place. A small rural Pennsylvania town in 1863, it gained fame first for the scale of the battle that occurred there and later for the words composed by Lincoln to commemorate the event. The scale of violence over the three days of fighting—almost 50,000 casualties between the two sides—was not surpassed in a single battle during the remainder of the war. Lincoln's November address immortalized the fallen soldiers and recast Northern effort in the war as the preservation of "government of the people, by the people, for the people."

The story of the battle has been told so many times it comes to seem inevitable, but the actual sequence points to the spontaneity and unpredictability of the event. Without the advantage of Stuart's intelligence and with limited knowledge of the local terrain, Lee's forces first encountered a significant Federal presence in the town of Gettysburg. Early on the morning of July 1, Henry Heth and Jubal Early's divisions encountered Federal cavalry in the town and engaged them. As the fight extended through the day, more men were drawn into the fight. Although Lee was uncertain about committing to a full battle, the sprawling conflict demanded additional resources. By late in the day, Confederates succeeded in pushing Union forces out of the town. Unfortunately, the Northern soldiers retreated onto the high ground of Cemetery Ridge south of Gettysburg. This would become the pivotal battle line over the coming days.

Buoyed by his success the day before, Lee attacked the Federal lines again on July 2. Meade had prepared for the attack and had dispersed his troops effectively along a fishhook-shaped line that began at Culp's Hill on the far right and extended down Cemetery Ridge and, by the end of the day, to a small wooded hill called Little Round Top. The Confederate attack on the Union left, led by Longstreet's Corps, had the most success. Confederates inflicted extraordinarily high casualty rates—famously felling 215 of the 262 members of the First Minnesota—on Daniel Sickles's troops fighting in the "Devil's Den" and a nearby peach orchard. They finally broke the Northern line but even the hand-to-hand fighting between Maine and Texas and Alabama troops could not dislodge the Union's position on Little Round Top.

The morning of July 3 opened with the Union forces arrayed in much the same position they had been the day before. Lee, with the same faith in his troops that had carried him through Antietam and Chancellorsville, planned another assault on the Federal lines. Delays, miscommunication, and a dispute between Longstreet and Lee about the wisdom of the attack slowed the Confederates, who when they came in the early afternoon, hit the middle of the Union line on Cemetery Ridge. Commonly known as Pickett's charge, over 12,000 troops from Longstreet's corps moved forward to meet Winfield Scott Hancock's corps. A Union soldier, well entrenched and backed by ranks of artillery, noted it was "Fredericksburg on the other leg," as he saw the tables now turned on the unlucky Rebels. A two-hour artillery duel did little to weaken Union defenses and when the attack finally came, Confederates were cut down by cannon and musket fire at a murderous rate. After nearly 5,600 casualties, Lee called off the attack.

Although desultory fighting continued on July 4, news flashed across the North that day trumpeting the repulse of Lee's second invasion of the North. Unlike Antietam, which ended with a stalemate, Meade could claim a true victory at Gettysburg, the first against Lee by a Northern commander. Combined with news of the fall of Vicksburg, the announcement helped revive sagging hopes and Republican fortunes in the North. If it is clear that the victory was essential for the North, it is not so clear that the battle represented a turning point in the war. Most Confederates interpreted the battle as a setback but only a temporary one. Lee retreated back into Virginia, but nearly two years of bloody fighting lay ahead.

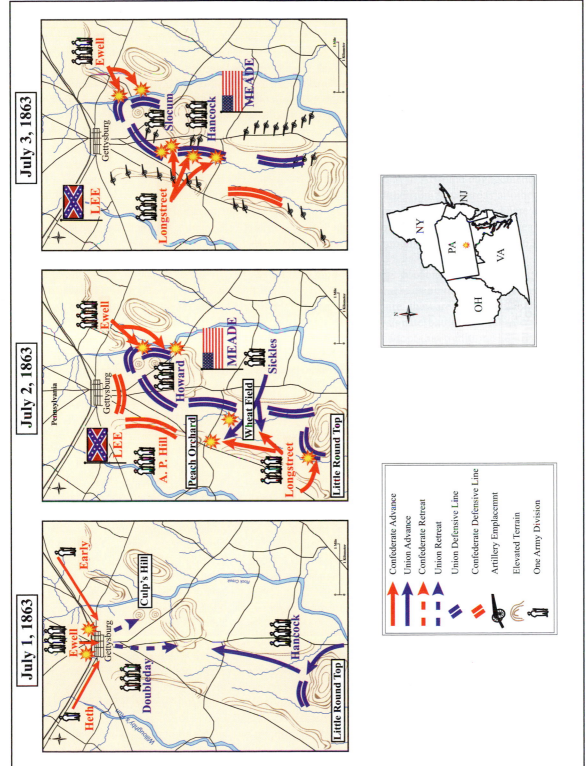

July 1, 1863

July 2, 1863

July 3, 1863

Heth
Ewell
Early
Culp's Hill
Gettysburg
Doubleday
Hancock
Willoughby's Run
Rock Creek
Little Round Top

Pennsylvania
LEE
Ewell
A. P. Hill
Peach Orchard
Gettysburg
Howard
MEADE
Sickles
Wheat Field
Longstreet
Little Round Top

LEE
Ewell
Longstreet
Slocum
Hancock
MEADE
Gettysburg

NY
NJ
PA
VA
OH
N

Confederate Advance
Union Advance
Confederate Retreat
Union Retreat
Union Defensive Line
Confederate Defensive Line
Artillery Emplacemnt
Elevated Terrain
One Army Division

30 DISSENT

Historians' long debate about which side possessed a more damaging opposition has generated greater insight into the nature of dissent in each section, though it has yet to answer the bedrock question. Opposition within the North coalesced around certain issues and within certain boundaries. As in the South, the draft inspired heated opposition. Many Democrats denounced conscription as unmanly and unconstitutional. Particularly after the North adopted emancipation as a goal, conservatives avoided or protested the draft as a means of protest against the war itself. Mayors and governors did their best to avoid having to implement the draft, preferring to offer enlistment bonuses and other incentives to attract recruits. Nonetheless, there were serious draft riots in cities all across the North, but particularly around southern New York, New Jersey, and eastern Pennsylvania. The worst episode occurred just after the battle of Gettysburg and consisted of a week of racial violence and mayhem in New York City. Begun as a draft protest by predominantly Irish and German immigrant dockworkers, the riot turned into a racial pogrom, with black men and women hunted down and lynched, the Colored Children's Orphanage burned to the ground, and the houses of leading city Republicans targeted for destruction.

Democrats asserted their innocence with regard to the riots but sympathized with the arguments of protesters. Within the national Democratic Party, some retained their party opposition but supported the war, a difficult balancing act for all but the most skilled politicians. Others, known as Copperheads, argued for an immediate end to the war and denounced Lincoln in violent terms. The most famous among these was Ohio congressman Clement Vallandigham, whose speeches calling for desertion and resistance to emancipation prompted his arrest by military authorities. Seeking to diffuse an ugly civil liberties issue, Lincoln had Vallandigham exiled to the Confederacy. The upturn in Northern fortunes in 1863 relieved some pressure, but Lincoln continued to face serious opposition until his death in 1865.

The Davis administration and the Confederacy faced equally serious opposition within the South. Unlike the North, where much dissent was channeled through the political system, the South abolished its party system. Opposition to Davis and other leaders thus became intensely personal and counterproductive to the war effort. Davis's aggressive nationalist policies angered civil libertarians, and many others complained about the unequal costs of waging the war. Draft exemptions for large slaveholders and the practice of substitution seemed to indicate a class bias in Confederate legislation that common people despised. Class conflict, as evidenced in Richmond's famous April 1863 bread riot—when local women protesting the high cost of flour and other staples were faced down by armed Confederate troops—presented a continuous problem for the Confederacy even though its aggregate effect is hard to calculate. Davis faced much of the same criticism as Lincoln, especially for his centralizing policies, which included taxes, impressments, and, eventually, a tax-in-kind. Both presidents suspended habeas corpus, both jailed political opponents, both restricted the press, and both fought off accusations that their actions were the work of tyrants.

The most serious opposition came from those parts of the South with substantial bodies of people loyal to the Union. Eastern Tennessee and western North Carolina were notorious Unionist strongholds. Residents of these regions did little to support the Confederate war effort, and in east Tennessee, actively aided the Union military cause. There were also pockets of deep resistance to Confederate authority that came from a mix of elements: prewar political Unionism, low slaveholding, wartime hardship, and other local factors. Jones County, Mississippi, Floyd County, Virginia, and Horton County, Alabama, all saw the creation of large deserter bands. These bands were composed of men who escaped from Confederate service and lived around the edges of their home communities. In some situations they drew on the support of friends and families, whereas in others they lived as bandits or criminal gangs who preyed on civilians.

Atlantic Ocean

Gulf of Mexico

Legend:
- Northern Draft Riots
- Areas of Copperhead Support
- Native American Conflicts
- Guerrilla Conflicts
- Areas of Unionist Support
- Confederate Deserter Conflicts

MAINE

Montpelier

Boston

NH

VT

MA

CT

Albany

NEW YORK

NJ

WASHINGTON, D.C.

MD

Richmond

PENNSYLVANIA

Harrisburg

Raleigh

NORTH CAROLINA

VIRGINIA

SOUTH CAROLINA

Columbia

OHIO

Columbus

Louisville

KENTUCKY

Nashville

TENNESSEE

Atlanta

GEORGIA

Tallahassee

FLORIDA

MICHIGAN

Lansing

INDIANA

Indianapolis

Ohio River

ALABAMA

Montgomery

ILLINOIS

Springfield

MISSISSIPPI

Jackson

WISCONSIN

Madison

Saint Paul

MINNESOTA

Des Moines

IOWA

MISSOURI

Jefferson City

ARKANSAS

Little Rock

Mississippi River

LOUISIANA

Baton Rouge

Missouri River

Topeka

Lincoln

NEBRASKA TERRITORY

KANSAS

OKLAHOMA TERRITORY

Arkansas River

DAKOTA TERRITORY

TEXAS

Dallas

Austin

N

31 THE VICKSBURG CAMPAIGNS

With control of Corinth and Iuka in northern Mississippi secured in the fall, Grant turned his attention to the last major Confederate bastion on the Mississippi River at Vicksburg. Grant launched his first effort in December 1862. Assisted by William T. Sherman, who would become Grant's most trusted lieutenant, Grant spent a fruitless month maneuvering around the northern section of the state. Confederate cavalry general Nathan B. Forrest and Van Dorn foiled Grant's efforts to mount a full campaign by disrupting his supply lines and destroying the main Union depot in the region at Holly Springs. The Vicksburg campaign proved one of the last episodes where Grant was stymied by supply line problems; in the future, he and Sherman would instruct their troops to live off the land rather than relying on lengthy and vulnerable supply trains.

In January 1863, Grant established his headquarters at Milliken's Bend, Louisiana. For the next six months, he labored unsuccessfully to find an attack route against Vicksburg, which sits on the Mississippi side of the river, bracketed by particularly tangled stretches of the river and protected to the west by long stretches of marshy ground unsuitable for launching an attack. Grant tried a variety of different approaches, including cutting new channels through the swamps and attempting an attack down the Tallahatchie River. As the months dragged on and his plans failed, critics of Grant suggested that his earlier victories had been flukes and that he was unfit to command owing to chronic alcohol abuse, but Grant's characteristic determination sustained him. Finally, on April 30, he marched his troops south on the western bank of the river, crossed over, captured Port Gibson, and launched a stunningly successful campaign that erased all doubts about his fitness to lead.

Vicksburg was ably defended by John C. Pemberton, who was closely monitoring Grant's progress. After crossing the river, Grant marched east toward Jackson, cutting off Pemberton's escape route if he decided to abandon the fort. Against hard fighting, Union troops pushed Confederates back in a series of battles to Jackson. Relying on Sherman and James B. McPherson, another trusted lieutenant, Grant then tacked back to the west toward Vicksburg. Pemberton had ordered troops out of the fort to slow Grant's advance but they were pushed back by mid-May. On May 19 and 22 Grant attacked the Confederate defenses and was repulsed with heavy losses both times. On May 25, he commenced a siege of the city, with Union artillery batteries lobbing thousands of shells into the city around the clock. Similar actions were taken against Port Hudson, farther to the south and positioned at a more defensible location. Vicksburg's soldiers and citizens alike took on a terrifying existence, living out of catacombs and bombproof shelters built into the hillsides around the city. Food grew scarce, until people were reduced to eating horses and mules. Finally, on July 4, Pemberton surrendered his remaining garrison of 29,500 men. Port Hudson surrendered several days later.

On July 9, Lincoln learned that, in his words, the "father of waters flows unvexed to the sea"; the United States once again controlled the entire length of the Mississippi River. This goal had been a Union war aim since the conflict's opening days and although Vicksburg's surrender was less dramatic (and less bloody) than Gettysburg, it was probably more important in strategic terms. With control of the river, the Union effectively cut the Confederacy in half, denying the movement of men and material from one side to the other. The Anaconda could now begin to squeeze.

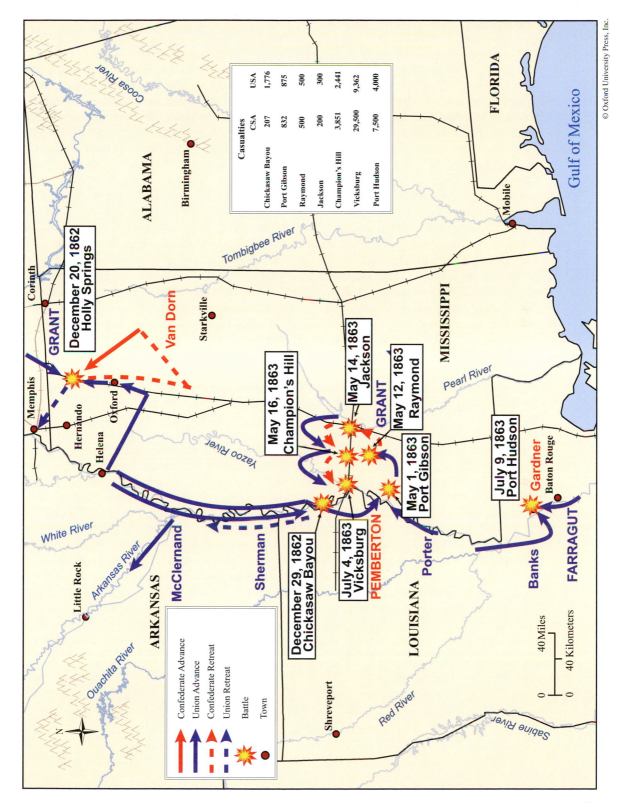

© Oxford University Press, Inc.

Casualties	CSA	USA
Chickasaw Bayou	207	1,776
Port Gibson	832	875
Raymond	500	500
Jackson	200	300
Champion's Hill	3,851	2,441
Vicksburg	29,500	9,362
Port Hudson	7,500	4,000

GRANT

December 20, 1862
Holly Springs

Van Dorn

May 16, 1863
Champion's Hill

May 14, 1863
Jackson

GRANT

May 12, 1863
Raymond

May 1, 1863
Port Gibson

PEMBERTON

July 4, 1863
Vicksburg

July 9, 1863
Port Hudson

Gardner

Porter

Banks

FARRAGUT

December 29, 1862
Chickasaw Bayou

McClernand

Sherman

ALABAMA

Birmingham

Tombigbee River

MISSISSIPPI

Pearl River

FLORIDA

Gulf of Mexico

Mobile

Corinth

Memphis

Hernando

Oxford

Helena

Yazoo River

White River

Arkansas River

Little Rock

ARKANSAS

Ouachita River

LOUISIANA

Shreveport

Red River

Sabine River

Baton Rouge

Starkville

Coosa River

Legend

- Confederate Advance
- Union Advance
- Confederate Retreat
- Union Retreat
- Battle
- Town

40 Miles

40 Kilometers

0

0

N

63

The bombardment and eventual capture of Vicksburg precipitated an exodus from the city, just as it had in Fredericksburg in December 1862 and other Confederate places before that. The people who left joined the flood of Southern refugees moving across the landscape in record numbers. The term "refugee" in its traditional meaning relative to the Civil War typically refers to white Confederates who fled in advance of the Union army. Under this definition, the most well-known first-wave refugees were those plantation owners along the South Carolina Sea Islands who abandoned the region when Union ships captured Port Royal. These well-to-do refugees generally moved to their second homes in Charleston and some later moved farther inland when the attacks on Charleston escalated in mid-1863. But the term "refugee" covers several other categories of Southerners, both white and black, both Confederate and Unionist, all of whom were dislocated by the process of war.

Refugeeing successfully required money and waves of wealthy Southerners chose to move rather than risk being caught up in the advance of Union troops. For instance, early in the war, Confederates from Alexandria moved south to Richmond. Wealthy refugees often moved in order to protect slavery property. They brought enslaved workers with them in the hopes of maintaining the institution in a different setting in the South. This was the case for Lucy Stone, a famous Confederate diarist, whose family left Vicksburg before Grant's arrival and moved into East Texas. As Stone observed, the costs of refugeeing could be high. During her flight, she noted that "all have lost heavily, some with princely estates and hundreds of Negroes, escaping with ten or twenty of their hands and only the clothes they have on." Stone's experiences in Texas demonstrated the tensions that often resulted from mass relocations, particularly among urbanites who moved to rural areas. Most poor people simply stayed where they were and hoped for the best. In fact, as most refugees learned to their sorrow, they often had a much better chance of keeping their property (if not their slave property) and their homes if they remained on their own land and dealt with Union soldiers face-to-face.

Even as pro-Confederates moved to escape the Union army, Unionist civilians often moved in the direction of the Union army. In areas of contested territory, like eastern Tennessee or southern Missouri, Unionists were often safer in garrison towns and so they moved to places like St. Louis or Knoxville, where Union provost guards controlled the public space. Often following this same pattern, but in even greater numbers, was the movement of African Americans within the South. The movement of freedpeople in the late stages of the war into urban areas controlled by the Union was an aspect of the war with profound consequences for the postwar period. Within Alabama, for instance, a large shift of freedpeople into Mobile in late 1864 and 1865 upset the political dynamics of African American life and the community as a whole well into the postwar period. Like the tensions among white residents, freedpeople came with different experiences and expectations from the free blacks who often congregated in antebellum southern cities. The movement of black people was further channeled through the Freedmen's Bureau Camps established along the Atlantic seaboard and along the major rivers. The political connotations attached to the word "refugee" in the twentieth century suggest a foreign concept for most Americans, but the people displaced by the violence and destruction of the Civil War prefigured more modern refugees in many respects.

Atlantic Ocean

200 Miles
200 Kilometers

© Oxford University Press, Inc.

WASHINGTON, D.C.
1862–65   Norfolk
1861–62
MARYLAND
1861–65   Richmond
VIRGINIA   Staunton
1864–65   New Berne
Raleigh
NORTH CAROLINA
1863–65
OHIO
1861–62   Knoxville
1863–65
KENTUCKY
Louisville   1862–65
Nashville
TENNESSEE
INDIANA
1861–65
St. Louis   1861–65
MISSOURI
1861–65
ARKANSAS
Memphis   1863–65   Little Rock
1862–65
1862–63
MISSISSIPPI   Vicksburg
1863–65
LOUISIANA   1862–65   New Orleans
TEXAS
SOUTH CAROLINA
Columbia   1863–65   Charleston
Savannah
1861
GEORGIA   Atlanta   1864–65
1863–65   ALABAMA
1864–65   Mobile   Pensacola
FLORIDA   1861–65
1864–65   Jacksonville   1862–65

IOWA

Confederate Refugee Movement
Unionist Refugee Movement
Town

65

33 TENNESSEE

In January 1863, in a battle that ended the Western campaign season as Fredericksburg had ended the Eastern one, Federals defeated Bragg's army at Stones River. Bragg was driven from central Tennessee and he entrenched himself outside Tullahoma. Rosecrans reorganized and rested his troops through the winter before launching them on a remarkably successful campaign. Rosecrans succeeded, largely through maneuver, in driving Bragg's army all the way to Chattanooga before entrenching his troops south of the city on Lookout Mountain. He did this at the same time that Meade and Lee devastated one another in Pennsylvania and Grant attacked Vicksburg. Rosecrans felt, probably justifiably, that his troops' accomplishment was overlooked because he incurred only a few hundred casualties. Bragg was as hesitant to engage as McClellan had been, much to the frustration of Jefferson Davis, but Rosecrans still deserves credit for a brilliant sequence of feints and movements that brought all of Tennessee under Union control by the end of August.

Once at Chattanooga, Rosecrans overplayed his hand. Assuming that Bragg's army was beaten and demoralized, he dispersed his own corps in different directions from the city. Bragg attacked and succeeded in trapping sections of the Union army along Chickamauga Creek. On September 19 and 20, the battle grew as both sides sent men into the fight. The battle of Chickamauga became the fiercest and most deadly of the Western theater. Bragg's army, reinforced by Longstreet's corps sent west by Lee, held the upper hand through the day and at one point broke the Union right entirely. Only a determined defense by Union general and Virginian George H. Thomas allowed the rest of the army to retreat into the safety of Chattanooga. In two days, the two sides produced over 34,000 casualties, but Bragg's success was marred by the safe retreat of Rosecrans back into the city.

Bragg settled into a slow siege of Chattanooga, occupying Lookout Mountain, immediately south, and Missionary Ridge, southeast of town. From these positions, Bragg reduced the flow of material into the city to a trickle and waited for Rosecrans to starve or try to break out. Grant was sent to the city, where he replaced Rosecrans with Thomas. At the same time, Bragg's army lost cohesion to internal disputes. Bragg also allowed Longstreet's corps to venture north, where they were decisively rebuffed in an attack on the Union garrison at Knoxville. In late November, Grant pushed his coordinated forces out of the city, first taking Lookout Mountain. On November 25, Thomas was ordered to make a demonstration in front of Missionary Ridge to allow other Union units time to attack from the sides. Eager to overcome the humiliation of Chickamauga, Thomas's Army of the Cumberland instead charged up the ridge, surprising the bunkered Confederates and scattering them from the mountain. Another inspired defense, this time led by Confederate general Patrick Cleburne, allowed the safe retreat of Bragg's broken army into northern Georgia, but the damage was done. Tennessee remained in Union hands for the remainder of the war. Bragg's army, weakened by dissension and complaints, came apart at the seams. Jefferson Davis made a highly unusual personal inspection of the army, after which he replaced Bragg with Joseph Johnston, to whom he issued instructions to keep the Union confined to northern Georgia. Much to Davis's anger, Johnston, replicating his performance on the peninsula in 1862, retreated all the way to Atlanta, giving Federals access to a rich agricultural region and allowing them to set up a siege of the city.

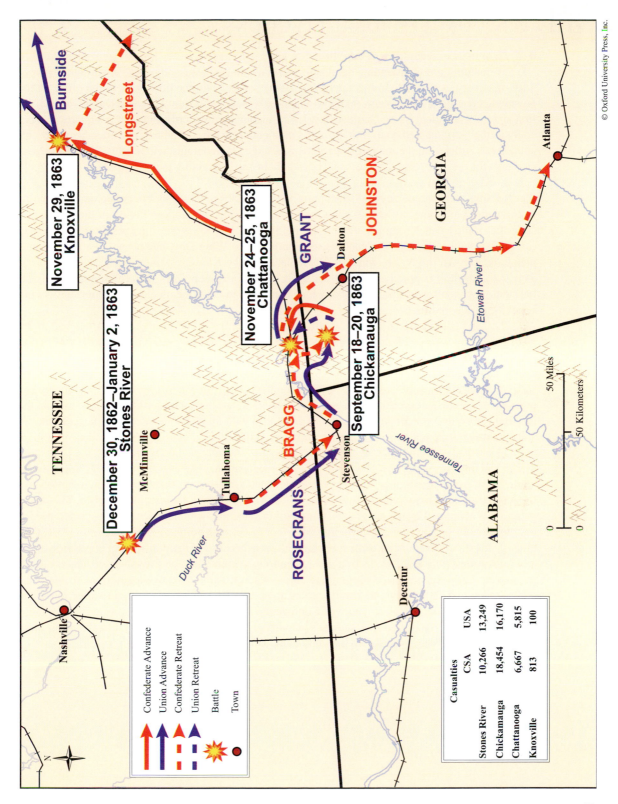

November 29, 1863
Knoxville

December 30, 1862–January 2, 1863
Stones River

November 24–25, 1863
Chattanooga

September 18–20, 1863
Chickamauga

Burnside

Longstreet

GRANT

JOHNSTON

GEORGIA

Atlanta

Dalton

Etowah River

BRAGG

ROSECRANS

Stevenson

Tennessee River

ALABAMA

Decatur

TENNESSEE

McMinnville

Tullahoma

Duck River

Nashville

© Oxford University Press, Inc.

50 Miles

50 Kilometers

0

0

Confederate Advance
Union Advance
Confederate Retreat
Union Retreat
Battle
Town

Casualties	CSA	USA
Stones River	10,266	13,249
Chickamauga	18,454	16,170
Chattanooga	6,667	5,815
Knoxville	813	100

34   C.S. CONGRESSIONAL ELECTIONS

When the Confederacy was established in early 1861, its founders largely replicated the U.S. Constitution in its founding document. Certain changes, especially those ensuring the perpetuity of slavery, were made immediately. Southerners also made modifications to the office of the president, creating one six-year term for which there was no reelection. Jefferson Davis was thus the first and only president of the Confederacy. Like Lincoln, he drew criticism from all quarters, especially as the North gained control of the war's momentum in the second half of 1863. Also like Lincoln, Davis suffered in the midterm elections, which the Confederates held in late 1863 (the official elections for president and Congress had been held in 1861, retaining the traditional two-year cycle but on odd years instead of even).

Because the Confederacy abolished party identifications in its attempt to create unity, the political dynamics are more difficult to chart than the Democratic-Republican divide of the North. Despite the official ban on parties, voters and politicians alike knew the lineages from which they came. The Democrats held dominance in the South, but the Whig Party had never collapsed as completely as it did in the North, where it was replaced by the Know-Nothings and then the Republicans. As a result, it is possible to chart the shifts in Confederate politics with reference to party labels that they themselves disavowed but which continued to color the ideological beliefs and voting behavior of congressmen.

The 1863 congressional elections were the first opportunity that Confederate voters had to express their displeasure with the course of the war. Despite the military gains made by the new nation up to this point, citizens had suffered serious hardship, rampant inflation, scarcity of goods, and the heavy hand of an increasingly strong federal government in Richmond. That popular anger could be seen in the election results; over half of the incumbent congressmen lost their seats, a stunning expression of dissatisfaction from the Confederate voters. It has been hard for historians to explain the election (or even Confederate politics more generally) with much greater precision because the results themselves are open to multiple interpretations. For instance, more Democrats than Whigs lost seats, even though Democrats, as the prewar party more firmly dedicated to protecting individual rights, had opposed aspects of Davis's centralizing legislation, such as the draft or the hated tax-in-kind. These congressmen may well have been defeated precisely for their opposition to nationalizing legislation that many citizens saw as the best hope of ensuring the nation's survival. This interpretation is supported by the geographic pattern of the election, which shows a strong preference for new leadership in parts of occupied Virginia, Tennessee, and northern Alabama and Georgia. In other districts, however, incumbents retained their seats because of their outspoken opposition to the administration's policies. The election was not entirely a referendum on Davis—the Congress itself, for instance, had been remarkably unimaginative when it came to crafting solutions to the challenges facing the nation—but the results served as a clear rebuke to the policies and direction of the war in late 1863. The turbulent nature of Confederate politics has led some historians to read these results as a sign of fatal divisions within the Confederacy while others see a political system more personalized but no less destructive than that in the Union.

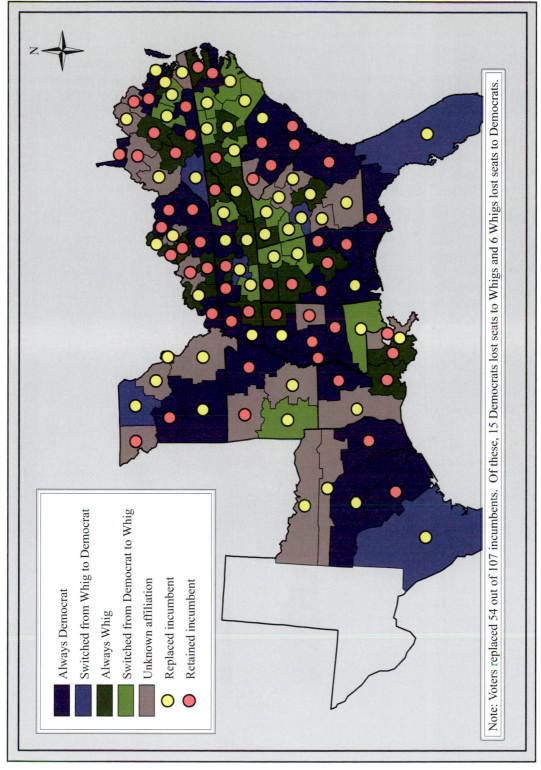

Note: Voters replaced 54 out of 107 incumbents. Of these, 15 Democrats lost seats to Whigs and 6 Whigs lost seats to Democrats.

Legend:
- Always Democrat
- Switched from Whig to Democrat
- Always Whig
- Switched from Democrat to Whig
- Unknown affiliation
- Replaced incumbent
- Retained incumbent

35 THE OVERLAND CAMPAIGN

After Lee's return to Virginia following Gettysburg in mid-1863, Meade followed, but the two sides fought only sporadically and the Union made no headway in its efforts to capture Richmond. Serious campaigning in Virginia only began again in May 1864, though this time with a new dynamic. Following Ulysses Grant's success at Vicksburg and then Chattanooga, Lincoln called him to Washington and promoted him to full command of the Union armies. Grant stayed in the East to oversee the campaign against Lee, although Meade remained in tactical command of the Army of the Potomac. Grant's old ally, William T. Sherman, assumed his role as ranking commander in the Western theater.

With Richmond and Lee's army still the main goals, Grant once again launched his army on the land route to the Confederate capital. The armies clashed first in the dense forests called the "Wilderness," near the previous year's battle of Chancellorsville. On May 5–7 the two sides inflicted heavy casualties on each other, nearly 30,000 total, with many wounded men consumed in fires that raged through the woods in the night. For soldiers listening to their comrades or enemies die in the flames, it was a grim start to what would be nearly six weeks of uninterrupted fighting with the equivalent in casualty terms of a battle of Bull Run every day. The fighting in the Wilderness produced little tactical change in the relation of the armies, but Grant moved south again, seeking a new advantage against Lee.

Both armies headed toward Spotsylvania Courthouse, but Lee's troops arrived first and quickly entrenched themselves. Grant and Meade attacked on the 10th and 11th, seeking a weakness in Lee's lines. The hardest fighting developed around a Confederate salient known as the "Mule Shoe," for its shape. On the morning of the 12th, Grant launched a massive attack on the salient, which temporarily broke the Confederate line, but the congested area became a sink. Men plunged into the area and fought in brutal hand-to-hand combat for twenty-two hours. Lee finally pulled his troops back from the now-christened "Bloody Angle," but the Union gained little by the victory. After more fighting, Grant turned his troops once again and proceeded south, demonstrating that he too understood what Lincoln called the "awful arithmetic" of the Union's numerical advantage. Crossing the North Anna River, Lee put up more resistance and again Grant pushed ahead. Union soldiers in the region, accustomed to a pattern of commanders who retreated after less damaging battles, developed a grudging admiration for Grant's persistence (as did many Confederates, still more grudgingly). Grant's one misstep, he later admitted in his memoirs, was ordering a frontal attack on a heavily entrenched Confederate position at Cold Harbor, where his soldiers fell in high numbers. Surveying the earthworks that they would have to attack the night before the battle, Union troops pinned their names and unit numbers to their uniforms in anticipation of their fate.

At the same time, Grant had ordered Benjamin Butler to proceed up the peninsula by water and attack Richmond from the east while Grant and Meade invaded from the north. Butler, with typical incompetence on the battlefield, inched along the peninsula despite heavily outnumbering Beauregard, who was placed in charge of the capital's defense with a handful of troops. Butler failed and only met up with Grant at Petersburg, where the latter had moved his troops in one last attempt to maneuver around Lee. Despite Grant's frustration with his failure to capture Lee's army or the capital, he succeeded in doing what previous Union commanders could not: pinning down his Confederate nemesis at Richmond for a siege Lee knew he could not win.

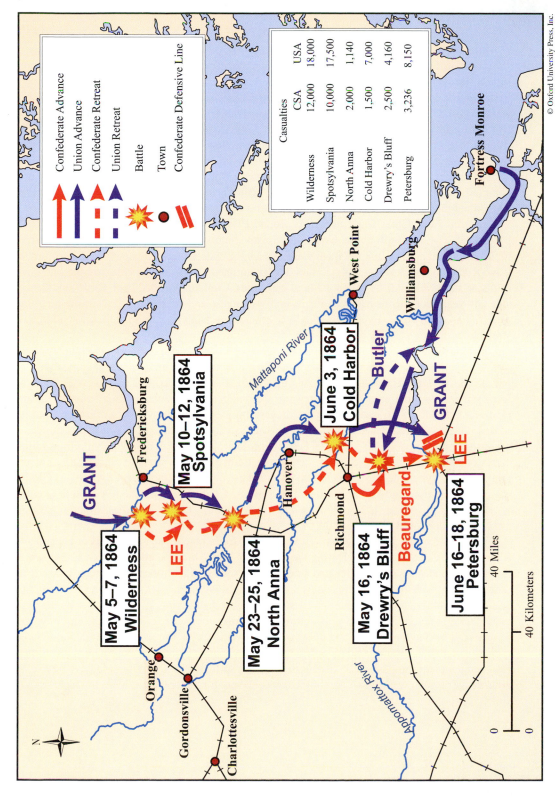

Casualties		
	CSA	USA
Wilderness	12,000	18,000
Spotsylvania	10,000	17,500
North Anna	2,000	1,140
Cold Harbor	1,500	7,000
Drewry's Bluff	2,500	4,160
Petersburg	3,236	8,150

Confederate Advance
Union Advance
Confederate Retreat
Union Retreat
Battle
Town
Confederate Defensive Line

May 5–7, 1864
Wilderness

May 10–12, 1864
Spotsylvania

May 23–25, 1864
North Anna

May 16, 1864
Drewry's Bluff

June 3, 1864
Cold Harbor

June 16–18, 1864
Petersburg

GRANT

LEE

GRANT

LEE

Butler

Beauregard

Fortress Monroe

West Point

Williamsburg

Fredericksburg

Hanover

Richmond

Orange

Gordonsville

Charlottesville

Mattaponi River

Appomattox River

40 Miles

40 Kilometers

N

© Oxford University Press, Inc.

36 PETERSBURG

Some historians have criticized Lee for his aggressive style of warfare. Both campaigns to the North, in 1862 and 1863, exacted high costs on the Confederacy in casualties, captives, and deserters. But both campaigns were successful in terms of reorienting the field of battle away from Richmond. Lee understood the advantages the Union possessed—more men, more and heavier weapons, and gunships in all the rivers. These advantages were lessened, if not nullified, when Northern armies were forced to march to meet Confederates at points they chose. Above all, Lee wanted to avoid being trapped in Richmond because then all the natural advantages of the Union would come into play and the war would become a mere question of time and tenacity. By June 1864, Grant had already proven his tenacity; even Confederate soldiers referred to him as "that dammed old bulldog." Now the question was whether he could capture the city before Northerners abandoned their support for the administration and perhaps the war.

By mid-June, Grant was entrenched around Petersburg, which functioned as the gateway to Richmond. The city, built on the banks of the Appomattox River, controlled a network of five railroads, including a vital link to North Carolina. Grant understood that capturing Petersburg would leave Richmond defenseless and he immediately initiated attacks on the Confederate lines. The assaults of June yielded little except Federal casualties. Confederates had been fortifying the city for as many years as Federals had been fortifying Washington and the result was a similarly strong ring of forts and earthworks. Eventually, the lines connecting and protecting Richmond and Petersburg stretched to more than fifty miles.

The most famous assault came on June 30, when Union engineers detonated an enormous pile of explosives placed in a tunnel dug under the Confederate lines. The Crater, as it came to be known, was a failure for the Union—soldiers swarmed into the hole created by the blast without sufficient foresight and became easy targets once the Confederates reorganized. Chief among these were black Federals, hastily pushed forward at the last minute and shot down with relish by Confederate troops. Grant's more well-reasoned strategy was to take advantage of his superior numbers and press the campaign south and west of Petersburg. During August and September, Grant initiated a series of attacks along the Weldon & Petersburg Railroad, which led into North Carolina, and the Petersburg & Lynchburg Railroad, which provided a crucial western link for the city. At Globe Tavern, Reams Station, and Poplar Springs, Federals and Confederates clashed. Although Grant could not dislodge Confederate troops, he forced Lee to continually extend his lines, something the Southern commander could ill afford to do.

Union and Confederate soldiers faced each other from trenches that in retrospect seemed an eerie foreshadowing of World War I. During the months of trench warfare, men on both sides grew impatient, bitter, and increasingly alienated from civilian society. Conditions were much worse for Confederates, who subsisted on increasingly limited rations—typically small allotments of rancid meat and stale cornmeal. Union soldiers, well supplied by ships arriving at ports on the peninsula, contended with boredom and lice. Snipers became the most serious foe for both sides, requiring soldiers to stay well hidden during even the most routine movements for fear of being shot. Despite soldiers' typical complaints about the rigors of life on the march, after months in the trenches most longed to resumed a mobile campaign. The siege lasted into the spring of 1865, straining the patience of Northerners eager for the war's end. Lincoln looked elsewhere for victories to salvage his fortunes.

© Oxford University Press, Inc.

Legend:

Confederate Advance	(red arrow)
Union Advance	(dark blue arrow)
Union Retreat	(dashed blue arrow)
Battle	(burst symbol)
Town	(dot)
Confederate Defensive Line	(red curved line)
Union Defensive Line	(dark blue curved line)

West Point

Pamunkey River

Chickahominy River

James River

Charles City Court House

September 29, 1864
Fort Harrison

City Point

GRANT

July 30, 1864
Crater

Norfolk & Petersburg Railroad

August 18–21
Globe Tavern

Gibbon

August 25, 1864
Reams Station

Weldon & Petersburg Railroad

Richmond & Petersburg Railroad

Petersburg

LEE

Appomattox River

Chesterfield

Richmond

Richmond & Danville Railroad

A. P. Hill

September 30, 1864
Poplar Springs Church

Dinwiddie

Petersburg & Lynchburg Railroad

Casualties		
	CSA	USA
Crater	1,500	3,798
Globe Tavern	1,600	4,455
Reams Station	720	2,742
Fort Harrison	2,200	3,327
Poplar Springs Church	900	2,889

N

0   10 Miles

0   10 Kilometers

37 SHENANDOAH VALLEY

As a part of Grant's master plan for Virginia in 1864, he instructed Franz Sigel to raid up the Shenandoah Valley as he was advancing toward Richmond. In previous years, Lee had used the valley as a screen for moving his army north and the rich meadows of the region had long provided grains for soldiers and civilians around the state. Grant intended to deny Confederates both military and logistical access to the valley. Sigel made it only as far south as New Market, where a motley force of regular army reinforced with young cadets from the Virginia Military Institute (VMI), stalled the advance. Grant replaced Sigel with General David Hunter, who advanced with a larger force into Lexington, where he ordered the burning of the VMI barracks and the home of Virginia's governor, John Letcher, before proceeding south. Sensing the danger, Lee detailed Jubal Early to Lynchburg. After a brief fight on June 17–18, Hunter retreated over the mountains into the security of western Virginia.

Hunter's retreat left Early free to advance down the valley with his army, enjoying their role as liberators. Early left the valley and swung north into Maryland, where he defeated Lew Wallace's troops at the battle of Monocacy, outside Frederick. Early's troops advanced to the ring of forts surrounding Washington and skirmished with local militia units. Although he never seriously threatened the capital, the presence of a Confederate army on the outskirts of Washington was yet another embarrassment for Lincoln in what was becoming another lackluster summer. Early fell back into Virginia and returned to the valley, but not before one last raid that gained reknown. At the end of July, he sent a cavalry detachment on a mission into Franklin County, Pennsylvania. His troopers demanded $100,000 in gold from Chambersburg, as they had from Hagerstown and Frederick in Maryland, to cover the costs of destruction done by Hunter in the valley. When the city could not produce the ransom, Early's soldiers burned the town, ensuring it immortality as the one Northern town sacked by Confederates.

Frustrated by Early's success and still concerned about the security of the valley, Grant detailed his most trusted cavalry lieutenant, Philip Sheridan, to contain Early's army for good. Sheridan was both a more aggressive and a more competent commander than Hunter, a difference Early learned to his peril. With Confederate forces separated in the Lower Valley, Sheridan attacked at Winchester and drove the Confederates from the field on September 19 and again at Fisher's Hill three days later. Both battles were lopsided Federal victories with Confederates uncharacteristically disorganized and dispirited on the field. Valley residents, accustomed to victories by their protectors in grey, were stunned to see the rapid reversal of Confederate fortunes. Sheridan set about systematically destroying valley grain stockpiles (though his actual destruction failed to meet the high standard set by Grant, who wanted "a crow traveling the length of the valley to have to carry its provender in its beak"), while Early bided a chance for revenge. He found it on October 19, when Confederate troops surprised and overran a Federal position along Cedar Creek. Sheridan, absent from the battlefield in the morning, returned at midday, rallied his troops, and destroyed Early's army. This battle signaled the end of Confederate resistance in the Shenandoah Valley. Although remnants of Early's army remained in the valley through the winter, Union control effectively lasted through the end of the war. Sheridan's victories boosted Lincoln's fortunes late in the fall and contributed to his reelection in November.

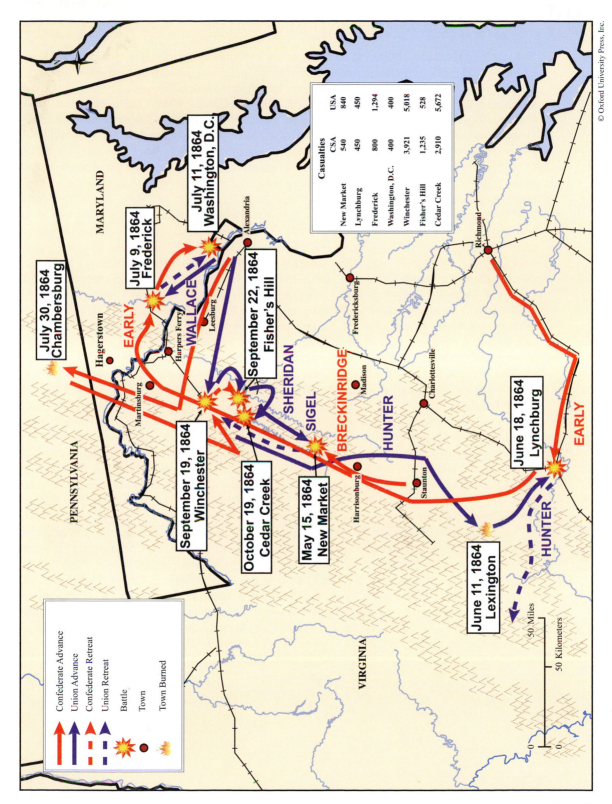

MARYLAND

July 11, 1864
Washington, D.C.

July 9, 1864
Frederick

Alexandria

July 30, 1864
Chambersburg

EARLY

WALLACE

September 22, 1864
Fisher's Hill

Hagerstown

Harpers Ferry

Leesburg

Fredericksburg

Richmond

Martinsburg

SHERIDAN

SIGEL

BRECKINRIDGE

HUNTER

Madison

Charlottesville

June 18, 1864
Lynchburg

EARLY

September 19, 1864
Winchester

October 19, 1864
Cedar Creek

May 15, 1864
New Market

Harrisonburg

Staunton

HUNTER

June 11, 1864
Lexington

PENNSYLVANIA

50 Miles

50 Kilometers

VIRGINIA

Confederate Advance
Union Advance
Confederate Retreat
Union Retreat
Battle
Town
Town Burned

Casualties	CSA	USA
New Market	540	840
Lynchburg	450	450
Frederick	800	1,294
Washington, D.C.	400	400
Winchester	3,921	5,018
Fisher's Hill	1,235	528
Cedar Creek	2,910	5,672

© Oxford University Press, Inc.

38 NAVAL CAMPAIGNS AND BLOCKADE

The Union blockade, initiated at the outset of the war, gained much greater strength in 1863 and 1864. The Union navy added hundreds of ships to its arsenal, most of them destined for blockade duty. The navy reorganized the venture into four separate blockading squadrons, each with responsibility for several major ports and hundreds of miles of coastline. Still, the blockade was never seamless. Tales abound about the fortunes made, a la Rhett Butler, by blockade runners who smuggled both valuable war supplies and expensive luxury products into the Confederacy. One of the key points of disagreement between the United States and Great Britain was the continuing construction of blockade runners by British shipbuilders. This problem came to a head in 1864 with the "Laird Rams," which looked as though they would have been a serious danger to the blockading squadrons before they were seized by the British government.

The extensive blockading fleet gave the navy the base from which to launch attacks on those few ports remaining open to the Confederacy. A combined naval and land campaign against Charleston in summer 1863, led by the black troops of the new Fifty-fourth Massachusetts, gained some ground for the Union but could not dislodge the Confederates from Fort Sumter, which sat at the entrance to the harbor. Despite intense shelling from Union gunboats, Charleston held out until a wing of Sherman's army attacked by land during the campaign north from Savannah in early 1865. A relatively unimportant port, Northerners yearned for Charleston's capture in revenge for its role as the incubator of secession. Of greater consequence was Mobile, which remained one of the last deepwater ports still in Confederate control in 1864. The naval campaign against Mobile Bay, led by Admiral David Farragut, took several weeks to execute owing to the network of coastal forts manned by Confederates and the Confederate ironclad *Tennessee* that patrolled the waters. The battle also saw the first use of a novel technology, known at the time as "torpedoes" (what today are called "mines"), placed in the water to slow the Union advance. When the first ship in Farragut's fleet hit one and immediately sank, the attack stalled, until Farragut famously called, "Damn the torpedoes! Full speed ahead." His ship safely maneuvered through the obstacles and eventually secured the capture of Mobile Bay (the city itself was not captured until early 1865). The August 23 announcement that the bay had fallen broke the long streak of bad news for the Union that summer. Lincoln's election was in deep peril (he thought it "unlikely") and the victory combined with similar Union accomplishments in the Shenandoah Valley and, most important, at Atlanta, helped bring him victory at the polls.

Although hard to calculate, there is little question that the blockade had an important effect on the Confederacy's ability to wage war. At the commencement of hostilities, Southerners saw their coastline as an asset—nothing so long could be effectively "closed." It took several years, but the Union did close the Confederate coast and forced its residents to subsist solely on what they could produce. With most white men in the armies, increasing numbers of slaves fleeing their plantations, and the general disruption of Union invasion, Southern farm productivity decreased during the war and this caused hardship for both civilians and soldiers. Although Northerners paid little attention to the blockade, the accomplishments of this facet of Northern policy fit perfectly into the evolving strategy of logistical devastation practiced by Grant and Sherman on land.

N

North Atlantic
Blockading Squadron

Note: by January 1865
the Federal Blockading
Squadron consisted of
471 ships.

South Atlantic
Blockading Squadron

Eastern Gulf
Blockading Squadron

Atlantic Ocean

250 Miles

250 Kilometers

0

0

© Oxford University Press, Inc.

Porter

Fortress Monroe

Cape Hatteras

Dahlgren

January 15, 1865
Fort Fisher

July–September, 1863
Charleston Harbor

Virginia

North Carolina

South Carolina

Jacksonville

Florida

Key West

August 22, 1864
Mobile Bay

Ohio

Indiana

Kentucky

Tennessee

Georgia

Alabama

Farragut

Illinois

Mississippi

Franklin

Western Gulf
Blockading Squadron

Union Advance
Union Retreat
Confederate Port
Union Port
Battle

Arkansas

Louisiana

New Orleans

September 8, 1863
Sabine Pass

Galveston

77

39 UNION OCCUPATION

One of the crucial factors in Northern victory was the increasing occupation of Southern territory. Occupation was also vital for distinguishing the experiences of Confederates and Federals. The latter perceived occupation as a return to normality while the former understood it as a humiliating ordeal. These varying perspectives would retain their significance well into the Reconstruction period. The most perceptive study of the experience of occupation identifies three types of occupation in the South: garrison towns, which were permanently occupied by Federal troops and thus economically and socially stable; frontier communities, which were exposed to periodic shifts of control and thus lived with more uncertainty; and the no-man's land, which was claimed by neither side but continually raided and overrun, leaving residents in a state of perpetual fear and confusion throughout the length of the war. Parts of central Virginia and central Tennessee fit the last model; in some communities, churches and other social entities effectively closed in 1861 and reemerged as functioning institutions only in 1865. The rim of occupied territory, including central Arkansas and northern Mississippi, functioned in frontier terms while cities like New Orleans and Nashville were garrison towns. The most unstable territory was in places at the edges of Northern control, such as eastern Tennessee and northern Alabama. The presence of Confederate deserter bands in these areas exacerbated the unsettled nature of the social order.

The geographic pattern of occupation reflects the success of Union arms over time. The North first stabilized control of those areas of slaveholding territory that remained within the Union, such as Missouri, Kentucky, and western Virginia. Next, they proceeded down the Mississippi River, establishing outposts on both sides of the river in order to control traffic up and down as well as across it. By the end of 1864, Union control extended in a thick line along the contours of the Mississippi as well as down the path followed by Sherman in his March to the Sea. The Union did not permanently occupy all the territory it invaded with the result that the areas occupied by the Union in 1862 but "behind the lines" by 1863 or 1864 were not subjected to uniform control throughout the whole remainder of the war. These places did not return to Confederate control but the citizenry within them might still have actively supported the Confederate war effort.

The intention of establishing Union control over Confederate territory was twofold: Federals wanted to assert control over the creation and movement of supplies that could aide the Confederate war effort, and the Union hoped to demonstrate to Southerners that their rights would be respected within the old system. Lincoln had the most success in this regard early in the war along the Lower Mississippi Valley. This area held some of the nation's wealthiest families and its largest plantations. With Butler's occupation of New Orleans in early 1862, the Union gave citizens north of the city the opportunity to return to the Union with slavery protected. Many of the planters in the area were conservative Whigs, well satisfied with the antebellum order. In addition, these planters were given nearly exclusive rights to sell cotton to Northern mill owners willing to pay any price. The combination of these incentives brought many planters back into the Union fold, but this experiment could not be replicated in other places. Most white Southerners supported the Confederacy and if they could not do so actively while living in occupied places or those frequented by the Union military, they tried to do so surreptitiously. One of the chief dangers for Union soldiers and for the success of the Union occupation in general was distinguishing serious threats from more political activities. In most occupied towns and cities, Union soldiers warily enforced order over disgruntled Confederate civilians who resented their presence and prayed for their exit.

Legend:

Union Military Posts

Confederate Cities (as of early 1865)

Occupied by Union at end of 1861

Occupied by Union at end of 1862

Occupied by Union at end of 1863

Occupied by Union at end of 1864

N

250 Miles

250 Kilometers

0

0

Washington, D.C.

Hatteras

Suffolk

Norfolk

Ft. Monroe

Plymouth

Beaufort

Romney

Winchester

Richmond

Raleigh

Fredericksburg

Gauley Bridge

Port Royal

Columbia

Savannah

Fernandina

Jacksonville

Frankfort

Milledgeville

Atlanta

Tallahassee

Louisville

Bowling Green

Knoxville

Chattanooga

Dalton

Rome

Huntsville

Nashville

Iuka

Tuscumbia

Montgomery

Ft. Henry

Ft. Donelson

Memphis

Corinth

Holly Springs

Cairo

Ft. Pickens

Mobile

Island No. 10

Little Rock

Helena

Vicksburg

Natchez

Baton Rouge

New Orleans

Rolla

Sedalia

Bentonville

Ft. Smith

Natchitoches

Alexandria

Sabine Pass

Galveston

79

40 BATTLES OF ATLANTA

After the Confederate defeat at Chattanooga in November 1863, Bragg's beaten army retreated into northern Georgia, where Jefferson Davis passed the command to Joseph Johnston. With Grant's promotion to lieutenant general and move to Washington, Northern forces underwent a similar reorganization. It was not until May 1864 when Sherman commenced his initiative against Johnston. From mid-May to early July, Union troops maneuvered and fought Confederates in a slow path south toward Atlanta. Sherman's command was composed of three separate armies, all under able commanders, and numbered nearly 100,000 men. Johnston, with 60,000 men, knew that he faced long odds in defeating Sherman. His main goal was to stall the Union advance, as Lee was doing in Richmond, long enough for Northerners to lose faith in the war or for Lincoln to lose the election.

Johnston had already demonstrated his skill at the strategic retreat and he maneuvered effectively once again. At each juncture, Johnston selected points of maximum defensibility and either forced Sherman to attack and incur casualties or spend time and energy maneuvering around him. Sherman grew frustrated and occasionally attacked prematurely, as at Resaca and Kennesaw Mountain, but he consistently found ways to flank and press Johnston to gain advantage. Part of Grant and Sherman's success hinged on their effective use of their numerical advantage, something that previous Union commanders had failed to do.

On July 9, Johnston withdrew into the confines of Atlanta and on July 17, Davis replaced him with John Bell Hood. Johnston had performed admirably given the circumstances, but Davis feared that retreat would depress Confederate morale and eventually compromise the security of Atlanta, the second most important Confederate city behind Richmond. Bell, a Texan and legendary brigade and then division commander in the army, was promoted because he fought aggressively. Understanding his charge, he attacked Sherman's army on the outskirts of the city within days. From July 20 to 28, Hood's troops targeted the various armies of Sherman's command, always inflicting damage but never the kind of knockout blow that Hood was seeking. Sherman regained the initiative in early August and began bombarding the city and isolating sections of Hood's defensive lines. Before attacking, Sherman directed the mayor to remove all civilians and in response to the mayor's protest, Sherman issued his explanation of the nature of the war, writing, "War is cruelty, and you cannot refine it; and those who brought war into our country deserve all the curses and maledictions a people can pour out." Sherman held out a solution, explaining that if white Southerners would "once more acknowledge the authority of the national Government . . . I and this army become at once your protectors and supporters, shielding you from danger, let it come from what quarter it may." By the end of the month, further defense was untenable and Hood withdrew his army. On September 2, a corps of Sherman's army entered Atlanta and Sherman wired Lincoln, "Atlanta is ours, and fairly won."

The victory came at a point when the war could have taken a drastically different direction than the one we recognize today. The Northern public, depressed at the seeming lack of failure on both the eastern and western fronts, was again nearly despondent. By mid-August, it was apparent to Lincoln that he would not be reelected and that George B. McClellan, the former Union general and current Democratic presidential candidate, would win with no obligation to sustain emancipation or even reunify the country. Sherman's victory at Atlanta can be fairly said to have won Lincoln reelection. Combined with the good news of Mobile Bay's capture and Sheridan's destruction of the Shenandoah Valley, Northern war fortunes seemed at last to be moving in the right direction. Nonetheless, it is important to recognize both how closely connected military and political fortunes were during the war and how variable were the attitudes of the publics in both sections.

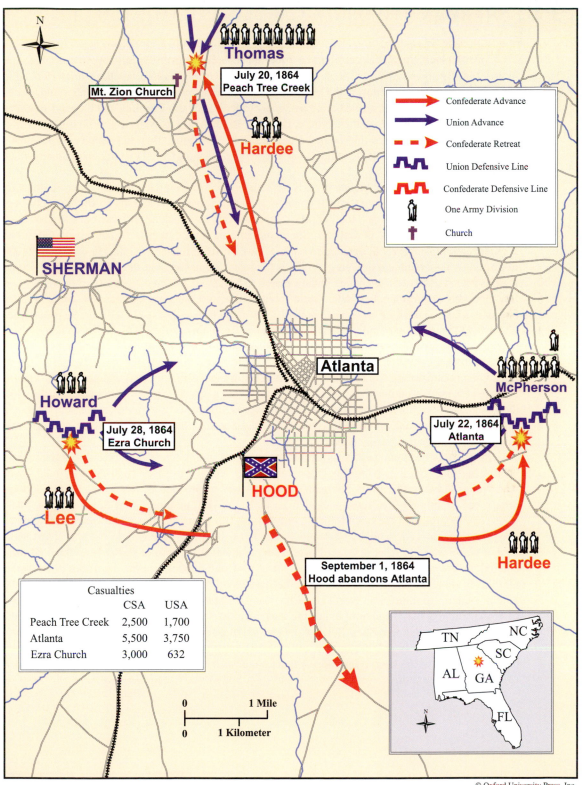

Thomas

July 20, 1864
Peach Tree Creek

Mt. Zion Church

Hardee

	Confederate Advance
	Union Advance
	Confederate Retreat
	Union Defensive Line
	Confederate Defensive Line
	One Army Division
	Church

SHERMAN

Atlanta

McPherson

Howard

July 28, 1864
Ezra Church

July 22, 1864
Atlanta

Lee

HOOD

Hardee

September 1, 1864
Hood abandons Atlanta

Casualties		
	CSA	USA
Peach Tree Creek	2,500	1,700
Atlanta	5,500	3,750
Ezra Church	3,000	632

0   1 Mile

0   1 Kilometer

TN   NC
               SC
AL   GA
          FL

© Oxford University Press, Inc.

41 Sherman's Georgia/Carolinas Campaign

William T. Sherman's "March to the Sea," when he shifted his base of operations from Atlanta to Savannah after Hood's departure from the state, has become of the one of the most infamous events of the Civil War. The destruction Sherman's troops caused has been immortalized in song, story, painting, and film, with Georgia earning a unique measure of the nation's sympathy. In fact, Sherman's soldiers destroyed more personal property in South Carolina and they did so with a relish generally missing from their time in Georgia. Strategically as well, it was Sherman's movement through the Carolinas that helped close the Civil War rather than his capture of Savannah. Nonetheless, the event has come to represent a style of warfare perfected by Grant and Sherman late in the war.

After Sherman entered Atlanta in early September, Hood recognized the difficulty of attacking him within the city. Hoping to draw Sherman out, Hood's forces attacked his northern supply lines that ran back to Chattanooga. Hood hoped to replicate this approach all the way back to Tennessee and deny Sherman control of Georgia. Sherman, building on the approach that he and Grant had been developing since 1863, decided to cut his army off from its supply line. He detached 40,000 troops under the command of George Thomas to protect Tennessee, but the main body of his army was instructed to "live off the land" in their march to Savannah. Given the paucity of opposition—a few thousand cavalrymen and state militia spread out across the state—it was not asking a lot of Sherman's battle-hardened veterans to both maneuver and forage. For many it became a pleasure, as it allowed them license to impose a hard war on those Southern civilians who had sustained the brutal war against them for the past many years. Research into the roots of the Union's policy of hard war reveals that common soldiers played a key role in its origins, both out of necessity (Union rations, though better than Confederates, were rarely sufficient on their own) and politics (Northerners expected nonslaveholders to welcome them and were angry when they did not). Sherman's soldiers marched east in four parallel columns, covering about sixty miles of the countryside and destroying war material and foodstuffs along the way. Sherman later admitted that a significant majority of the destruction was "simple waste."

Sherman's troops entered Savannah on December 21 and he presented the city to Lincoln as a "Christmas gift," but they paused only long enough to detach the tens of thousands of freed slaves who were following the army. Sherman's real goal was to proceed across the Carolinas and approach the Richmond-Petersburg theater from the southwest, helping Grant finish off Lee. Sherman's soldiers relished the opportunity to enter South Carolina. "Here is where secession started," one private announced, "and, by God, here is where it will end!" When Charleston was at last liberated, it was a troop of African American soldiers, many of them former slaves from the area, who entered the town first, a special indignity to the city's Confederates. Sherman's troops did not start the fires that consumed most of Columbia, the state capital, but neither did they labor to stop them. Union soldiers continued into North Carolina where, in March 1865, they dispatched the remnants of Hood's Tennessee army, now under the leadership of Joseph Johnston. Sherman intended his marches to impress upon Deep South Confederates the inability of their government to protect them, and this it surely did, but there is little evidence that the marches inspired white Southerners to relish a return to the Union. Instead, evidence suggests that the Union's hard war only embittered Confederates even more.

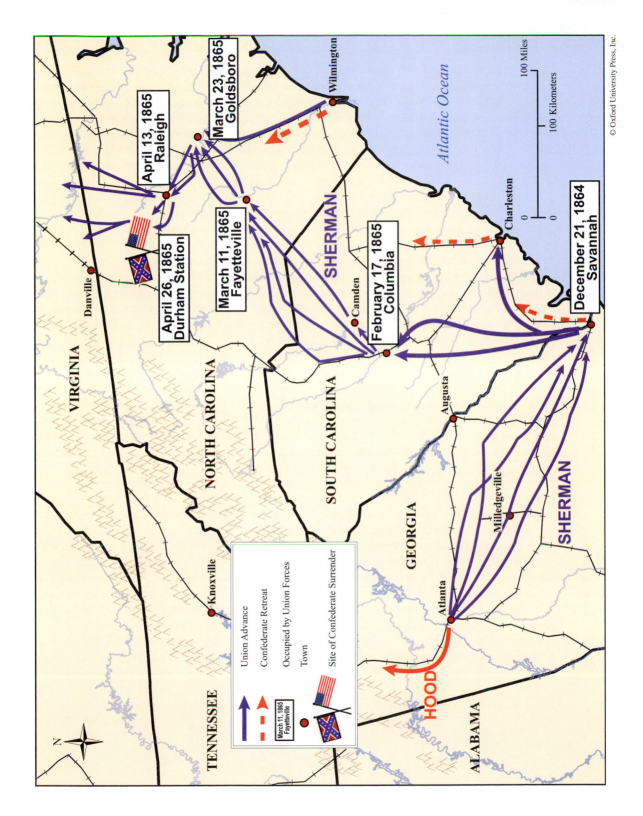

Atlantic Ocean

March 23, 1865
Goldsboro

April 13, 1865
Raleigh

April 26, 1865
Durham Station

March 11, 1865
Fayetteville

February 17, 1865
Columbia

December 21, 1864
Savannah

SHERMAN

SHERMAN

HOOD

VIRGINIA

NORTH CAROLINA

SOUTH CAROLINA

GEORGIA

TENNESSEE

ALABAMA

Wilmington

Charleston

Danville

Camden

Augusta

Milledgeville

Atlanta

Knoxville

100 Miles

100 Kilometers

Union Advance
Confederate Retreat
Occupied by Union Forces
Town
Site of Confederate Surrender

March 11, 1865
Fayetteville

N

© Oxford University Press, Inc.

42 CONTRABAND CAMPS

By the time of Sherman's march, the Northern policy toward freed slaves was well established: the armies liberated slaves as they marched through the South, relied on the slaves for information, occasionally enrolled black men and women as laborers or cooks, and tried to prevent large populations of freedmen, as they were referred to, from attaching themselves to the armies. When Sherman reached Savannah, he convened a meeting with local African American ministers and discussed plans for the postwar period. In Special Field Order No. 15, Sherman provided for the settlement of 40,000 freedpeople on the Sea Islands and coastal plain of South Carolina, Georgia, and northern Florida. This amounted to a massive redistribution of some of the most valuable land in the United States, and President Johnson later helped restore ownership to the whites who controlled the area before the war. Sherman's cavalier manner reflected something of the ad hoc nature of Northern policy toward freed slaves during the war. Lincoln's Emancipation Proclamation had been designed to deny a resource to the Confederacy but, other than providing for the enrollment of black men in Union forces, did not anticipate how the North would manage emancipation.

The problems began before the proclamation was ever announced. The first slaves to escape to Union lines did so in the war's opening month, when three men presented themselves to General Butler at Fortress Monroe. His policy of declaring them "contraband" solved the problem in legal terms, but many Democratic generals were uneasy with emancipation and returned runaway slaves to their masters. The issue pressed itself on the Northern public in the wake of Grant's invasion of Tennessee in 1862. Following his successes in the western part of the state, thousands of slaves moved to the safety of Federal lines. His officers began quarantining these people in "contraband camps," established near Federal military posts. Although these camps supposedly provided for the employment of freedpeople (as cooks and laundresses for the troops), living conditions were horrible. Reports of malnutrition, poor housing, and high rates of disease, as well as gross abuse by white Northern soldiers, proliferated in the press, and Grant was forced to appoint a deputy whose sole job was to clean and organize the camps.

The method established under Grant became a model for other commanders. In the future, military housing was provided and minimum wages were provided for work done to support the Northern war effort. By late 1862, Northern missionaries were entering the camps to help manage and instruct the ex-slaves. Literacy was the primary goal for people of all ages, and many Northern abolitionists saw this work as a natural extension of their prewar efforts against the slave system itself. The camps proliferated wherever the Union established a permanent presence. It remains difficult to gain a sense of the numbers of ex-slaves who spent time in the camps. Some camps were temporary and freedpeople were often shifted from one to another, so individual camp censuses (carried out, in any event, only by very scrupulous officers) do not necessarily add up to accurate aggregate numbers. The closest student of the process puts the total number at a quarter of a million people who lived in the camps at some point, or about one-third of all escaped slaves. Regardless of figures, the camps served as a crucial, and often unpleasant, transition to freedom for many African Americans and introduced many white Americans to the reality that the Federal government would help restructure the New South.

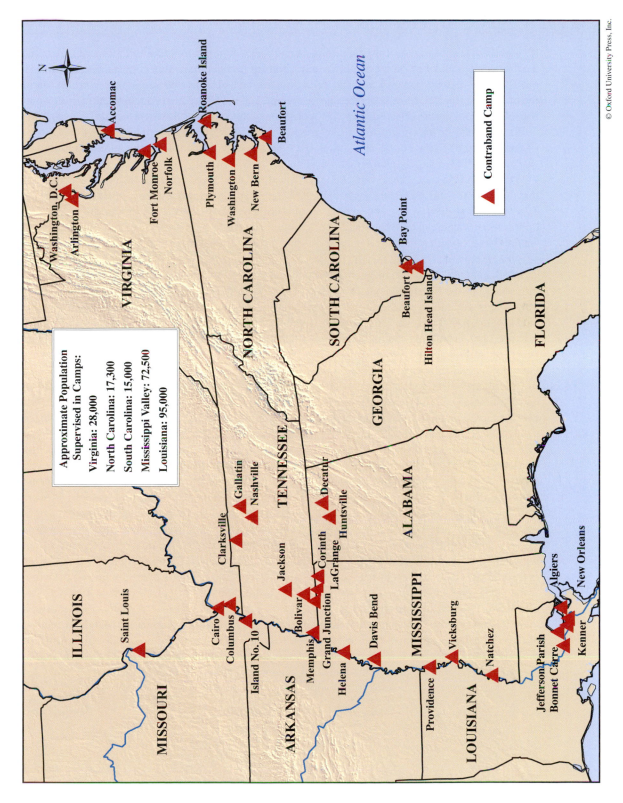

© Oxford University Press, Inc.

Atlantic Ocean

Approximate Population Supervised in Camps:
Virginia: 28,000
North Carolina: 17,300
South Carolina: 15,000
Mississippi Valley: 72,500
Louisiana: 95,000

Contraband Camp

N

VIRGINIA
NORTH CAROLINA
SOUTH CAROLINA
GEORGIA
FLORIDA
ALABAMA
TENNESSEE
MISSISSIPPI
LOUISIANA
ARKANSAS
MISSOURI
ILLINOIS

Accomac
Roanoke Island
Washington, D.C.
Arlington
Fort Monroe
Norfolk
Plymouth
Washington
New Bern
Beaufort
Bay Point
Beaufort
Hilton Head Island
Gallatin
Nashville
Decatur
Huntsville
Clarksville
Jackson
Corinth
LaGrange
Saint Louis
Cairo
Columbus
Island No. 10
Bolivar
Grand Junction
Memphis
Helena
Davis Bend
Vicksburg
Natchez
Providence
Bonnet Carre
Jefferson Parish
Algiers
New Orleans
Kenner

85

43 U.S. CONGRESSIONAL ELECTIONS

Despite the appearance of overwhelming Republican dominance in the fall 1864 elections, the outcome could well have been different. Abraham Lincoln knew this perhaps better than anyone. Long vilified by both radicals and conservatives, he had nearly been dumped from the top of the ticket in spring 1864, when his treasury secretary, Samuel Chase, made an open bid for the nomination. Lincoln outmaneuvered his rivals within the party but his ultimate reelection hinged on the military success of his commanders. Congressional Republicans saw their fortunes wax and wane as well, based upon the course of fighting, but with more detachment from the administration they succeeded or failed largely on their own account.

The 37th Congress, elected in 1860 and seated in December 1861 (as was usual according to the nineteenth-century schedule) was majority Republican but achieved its dominance thanks to the exit of Southern representatives, almost all of them Democrats. Secession produced much lower quorum requirements and Republicans took full advantage to pass a series of bills that had been stalled by sectional politics for a decade or longer. Chief among these was a plan to construct the first transcontinental railroad line, a goal sought by Illinois senator Stephen Douglas for much of his career. Republicans had also been championing a homestead act, land-grant college legislation, and in response to the fiscal demands of the war, a new banking act. These pieces of legislation, some long sought and others new to the war years, all reflected long-standing Republican, and in many cases, Whig, principles. The war provided Republicans with unprecedented opportunities for enacting their agenda but did not significantly alter that agenda. Northern Democrats, like their Southern peers, generally opposed Republican policies, seeing the work of the 37th Congress as too consolidating of federal authority.

Northern voters appear to have thought otherwise; they supported Republican candidates in record numbers in 1864. In part, this reflected the Republicans' campaign savvy in making the election a referendum on the war. After the disastrous midterm elections in 1862, Republicans organized a much more effective campaign machine that tied patriotism to electoral support of their party. Some War Democrats could protect themselves from attacks along these lines, but the rhetoric of the national party gave Republicans ample opportunity to contrast their support of the soldiers and the war effort to Democrats' weak-kneed response. The culmination of this came in the 1864 Democratic Platform, which seemed to put an end to the fighting above even the requirement of reunion. To many soldiers, including McClellan himself—who probably lost the loyalty of most of his former charges when he accepted the nomination—the platform repudiated the sacrifices already made by Northern soldiers on behalf of reunion. Democrats had greater success playing the race card, which they did with unbridled enthusiasm in 1864. Long enemies of emancipation, Democrats predicted the influx of millions of black workers to steal jobs and wives from Northern white men. Coining a new word, "miscegenation," Democrats unabashedly tried to scare Northern voters away from Lincoln. The effort failed and Republicans trounced Democrats at polls all across the North. Democrats retained a token presence in the 39th Congress, retaining seats in southern Illinois, Kentucky, Maryland, and the nucleus of Democratic opposition in New York City and its surrounding area. This alignment had profound importance for Reconstruction, as it was this Republican-dominated Congress, seated in December 1865, that engineered the transition to a more vigorous Reconstruction.

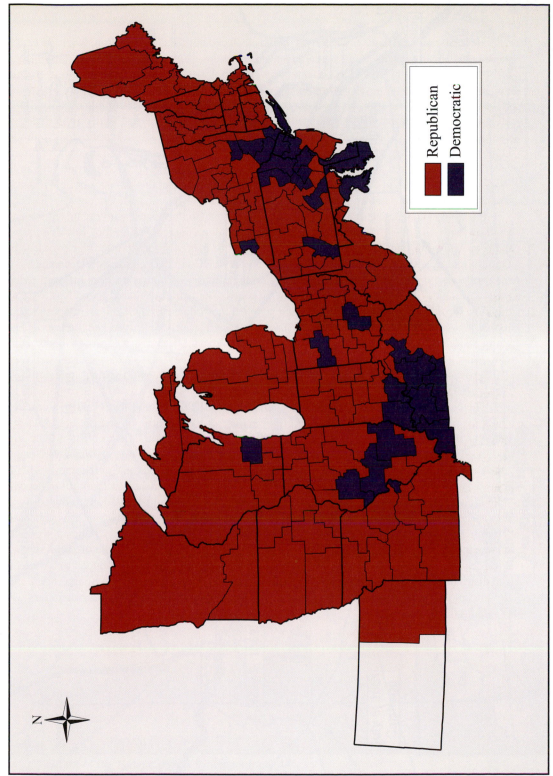

44 | Tennessee

After abandoning Atlanta to the Union, Hood advanced north as far as Dalton, where he captured a small Union garrison. Sherman advanced far enough to prevent Hood from destroying the railroad and forced the Confederates to move west into Alabama. Hood's plan was to liberate central Tennessee and then move east to join Lee outside Richmond. For the Union's part, Sherman detached George Thomas from his Georgia force and gave him 55,000 men to guard Nashville. The majority of these troops were already in the garrison town, with the rest under John Schofield's command at Columbia. Hood advanced rapidly and after failing to catch Schofield at Spring Hill, launched a bloody front assault on the Union line at Franklin. The result was a disaster for the Confederates, who incurred almost three times the casualties of the Federals. Confederate veteran Sam Watkins recalled the battle as "the grand coronation of death." After the battle, Schofield moved his troops quickly to join Thomas's command at Nashville.

Freezing rain and scant rations further weakened the Confederates, who organized for an assault on Nashville in early December. Some of his men were marching barefoot, but Hood pressed them on believing that discipline would enable them to prevail in any battle. Under orders from Grant, Thomas advanced out of Nashville first, driving the Confederates back on December 15 and then following up the next day. Despite being on the offensive, Thomas's forces inflicted twice as many casualties on the Confederates as they sustained. The battles at Franklin and Nashville were the most lopsided in the Western theater and signaled the collapse of the Confederate war machine in that region. When the battle ended, Hood's army was effectively destroyed and the last organized Confederate resistance in the Western theater ceased to exist. The few thousand of Hood's soldiers who remained were transferred east and reorganized under Johnston to resist Sherman's advance. This proved illusory, though with his adept maneuvering Johnston avoided final defeat until late April, after Lee had surrendered at Appomattox.

The condition of Hood's army after its defeat at Nashville mirrored that of many Confederate civilians. Tired, hungry, and frustrated with the failure of their enormous sacrifice to produce the outcome they expected, many Confederates prepared themselves for the final defeat of their armies and the end of their national experiment. This is not to say that Confederate civilians were eager to rejoin the Union. Aside from those diehard Unionists who had opposed the Confederacy throughout the war, few white Southerners, no matter their present hardship, relished the thought of becoming fellow citizens of their hated enemies. Grant's strategy of logistical devastation produced impressive successes for the Union in 1863 and 1864 and eventually helped win the war. It made possible reunion and secured the permanence of emancipation, but like most military policies it produced unanticipated consequences. In this case, the hard war policy inhibited the kind of social reconciliation that would make the peace truly productive. The North's hard war produced only bitterness and distrust among white Southerners. When this attitude combined with white Southerners' antipathy toward the recently freed slaves after the war, it provided an inauspicious foundation on which to rebuild the Union.

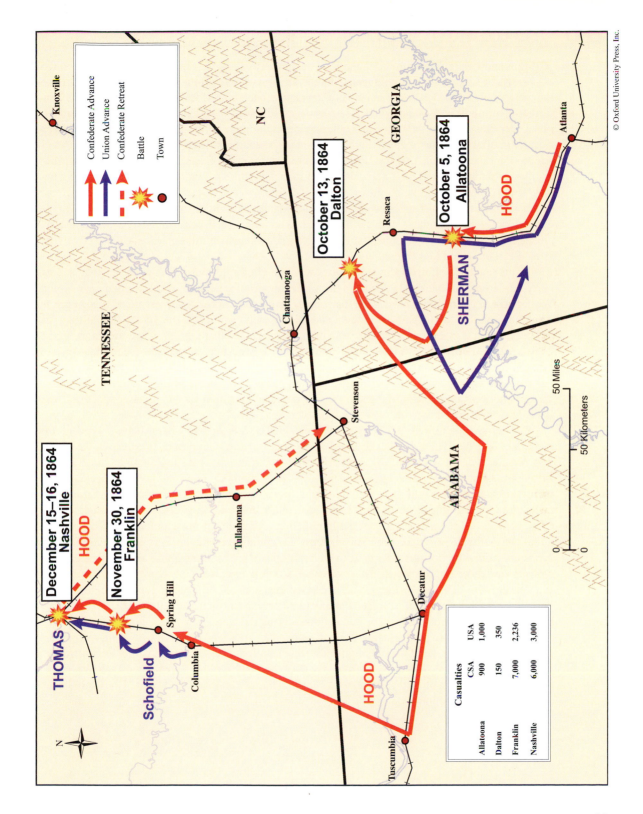

Knoxville

NC

GEORGIA

Atlanta

Resaca

October 13, 1864
Dalton

October 5, 1864
Allatoona

HOOD

SHERMAN

Chattanooga

TENNESSEE

Stevenson

50 Miles

50 Kilometers

ALABAMA

December 15–16, 1864
Nashville

HOOD

November 30, 1864
Franklin

Tullahoma

Decatur

Spring Hill

THOMAS

Schofield

Columbia

HOOD

Tuscumbia

Casualties	CSA	USA
Allatoona	900	1,000
Dalton	150	350
Franklin	7,000	2,236
Nashville	6,000	3,000

N

Legend:
Confederate Advance
Union Advance
Confederate Retreat
Battle
Town

45 APPOMATTOX CAMPAIGN

Grant and Lee remained mired in the mud outside Petersburg through the winter of 1864–1865. News of Atlanta's fall discouraged Confederates but only reinforced the importance of protecting the capital and the last major manufacturing center in the South. The destruction of Hood's army further dispirited Lee's soldiers, and deserters began slipping out of Lee's lines in January and February, some escaping to the Union and others returning to their homes throughout the South. Grant was continuing his strategy of extending his men to the south and west around Petersburg in an attempt to cut the railroads that sustained the Confederate capital. Lee saw the imminent collapse of his lines, stretched thin as they were. Hoping to force Grant momentarily back, Lee launched an attack at Fort Stedman on the northeast side of Petersburg. Though temporarily successful, Grant's forces pushed the Confederates back. Seizing the opportunity, Grant launched attacks all along the Confederate line. Sheridan's cavalry, supported by columns of Federal infantry, moved west and crushed George Pickett's command at Five Forks. This maneuver allowed Grant to effectively encircle Petersburg and Lee ordered his troops out.

Word reached Jefferson Davis while he was attending religious services on April 1, and his hasty exit from the church signaled to fellow parishioners the demise of the Confederate capital. While most white civilians barricaded themselves inside their homes, workers raced to package up what they could of the federal government and ship it south toward Danville on the last railroad line left open to the Confederacy. The city was officially evacuated that night, leaving fires burning that consumed much of the downtown, and Union forces moved immediately to occupy it. Abraham Lincoln traveled to the city by steamer on April 4 and was greeted at the wharf by thousands of African Americans, whose overwhelming public presence in the capital of the South's would-be slave republic made manifest the end of the Confederacy. White residents remained indoors, anxious to see how they would be treated by the occupying army.

Lee moved his army west, hoping to reach Amelia Courthouse, where much-needed rations were due to arrive. The Federals advanced to the south of Lee's army and cut off both the rations and any hope for escape to North Carolina. Desertions, captures, and simple fatigue drained thousands of men from Lee's army during the retreat from Richmond. Battles at Sayler's Creek and Farmville bled Lee's army still more and by April 9, it was apparent that he could fight no more. Lee contacted Grant to discuss terms of surrender. Grant's delivery of 25,000 rations to the starving Confederates was a generous act but the humiliation of defeat left few Confederates eager for reunion. The official surrender occurred on April 12, ending the war in Virginia. Although Joseph Johnston's army did not surrender until April 26, for many people, both North and South, Lee's surrender marked the end of the war. The coda came two days later, with the assassination of Abraham Lincoln in Ford's Theater by the famous Shakespearean actor John Wilkes Booth. Northerners' relief at the war's end on April 12 turned quickly to bitterness and anger with the murder of their president. Despite the fierce criticism he had suffered during the war, the North's success and Lincoln's murder elevated him to martyr status. Many Confederates mourned his passing as well, recognizing in his second inaugural call for "charity for all" that he might oversee a more gentle Reconstruction than Southerners once feared. Northern anger over the death of "my captain," in Walt Whitman's words, and the ascension of the Tennessee Unionist Andrew Johnson to the White House predicated a dark and uncertain future.

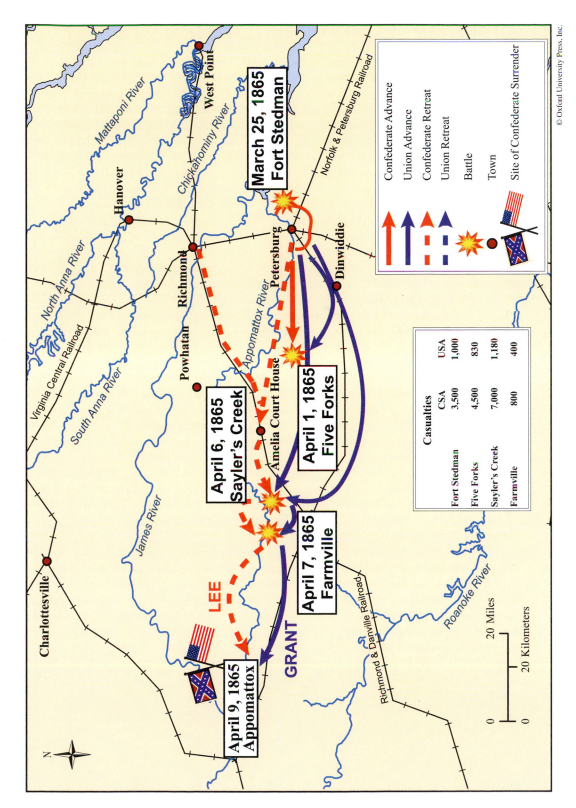

March 25, 1865
Fort Stedman

April 1, 1865
Five Forks

April 6, 1865
Sayler's Creek

April 7, 1865
Farmville

April 9, 1865
Appomattox

LEE

GRANT

West Point

Hanover

Richmond

Petersburg

Dinwiddie

Powhatan

Amelia Court House

Charlottesville

Mattaponi River

Chickahominy River

North Anna River

South Anna River

Virginia Central Railroad

Appomattox River

James River

Norfolk & Petersburg Railroad

Richmond & Danville Railroad

Roanoke River

Casualties		
	CSA	USA
Fort Stedman	3,500	1,000
Five Forks	4,500	830
Sayler's Creek	7,000	1,180
Farmville	800	400

Confederate Advance
Union Advance
Confederate Retreat
Union Retreat
Battle
Town
Site of Confederate Surrender

20 Miles
20 Kilometers
0   0

N

© Oxford University Press, Inc.

46 | BLACK POPULATION IN THE UNITED STATES

The most serious challenge facing the Union at the conclusion of the war was the future role of the freedpeople in the life of the nation. The Emancipation Proclamation had issued a sweeping grant of freedom across most of the Confederacy, but in practice, freedom came only where the Union army could accomplish and sustain it. It was thus only with the cessation of hostilities that full freedom reached those parts of the South that Union armies had not reached. "Juneteenth" was designated a holiday by African Americans to commemorate the date, June 16, 1865, when the news of emancipation reached the far western sections of Texas, where local planters had ignored the war's end and kept their slaves in bondage. Even slavery's death in west Texas did not end the institution nationally. In one of the war's bitterest ironies, Kentucky, a slaveholding Union state, did not emancipate its slaves until forced to do so at year's end by the Thirteenth Amendment. Missouri, Maryland, and Delaware, the other slaveholding states that remained loyal, all incorporated emancipation provisions into their state constitutions during the war, but Kentucky could not be budged. It served as telling proof that, just as Lincoln had predicted at the war's outset, slavery would be more secure in the Union than out of it. Despite his conservatism on the issue, Lincoln pushed hard for the adoption of the Thirteenth Amendment, recognizing the necessity of a permanent settlement of the issue beyond the wartime exigency of his proclamation.

The resistance of white Kentuckians aside, freedpeople embraced their new life with vigor. The day of Jubilee, as many called it, brought forth a release of emotion and energy literally hundreds of years in the making. The first act of most ex-slaves was to reestablish family bonds broken under slavery. This often entailed movement around the South, another freedom that had been denied slaves. The mass migration of black southerners during the postwar years unsettled white southerners and upset local economies. Hundreds of thousands of black men and women applied for marriage licenses, certifying in law unions that had existed in fact for years before emancipation. The state's certification of marriage also brought clear parentage rights over children, undoing one of the central crimes of the slave regime. Even with the reestablishment of families and the uncertainty surrounding future employment, most African Americans remained in the South. In 1880, the vast majority of African Americans lived in roughly the same places that their grandparents did, albeit with more people shifting west to the new cotton land of the Mississippi Delta and Tex-Arkana regions. The distribution of blacks within the nation did not change significantly until the second decade of the twentieth century, with the advent of the Great Migration to northern factory towns by Delta and other Deep South residents.

More complicated, and economically sensitive issues, resisted immediate solution. Northerners and southerners, black and white, struggled over a host of questions related to the freedpeople: What kind of work would they do? For what kind of wages? How would their entry into the labor markets affect white workers and salaries? How would the freedpeople be educated? Who would pay for that education? What would be their political role? Would they be allowed to vote? Reconstruction was the work of answering these questions and this work consumed the nation for three times as long as the war itself had lasted.

Less than 2% black residents

3–10% black residents

11–25% black residents

26–50% black residents

51%+ black residents

Territories (no census data)

47 MILITARY RECONSTRUCTION DISTRICTS

In March 1867, the Republican-led Congress passed the Reconstruction Acts. This legislation divided ten of the former Confederate states into five military districts, each under the control of a military governor (all Union generals), and established the terms by which they would be allowed reentry into the union. The Reconstruction Acts signaled the start of what historians today call Congressional Reconstruction and marked an escalation from the measures taken by President Andrew Johnson in the previous two years.

Johnson attempted a quick Reconstruction of the Confederate states. In mid-1865, he ordered new state and local elections, anticipating that voters would select "good men" and that these representatives would rejoin the Federal Congress, officially ending the enactment of secession in 1861. White southerners, emboldened by his generous terms, reelected many of those men who had led them during the war; former Confederate vice president Alexander Stephens, for instance, was elected senator from Georgia. Congress refused to seat these delegations and this inaugurated open hostilities with President Johnson. Northern anger was further stoked when the new southern state governments passed "black codes," statutory restrictions on the rights of African Americans. Many northerners saw in the laws, particularly those that apprenticed black children out to former masters, an intent to reestablish slavery. Republicans in Congress battled with Johnson over these issues for the next year and half, with most moderates growing more supportive of bolder efforts to ensure that emancipation included a modicum of protections for the freedmen, and equally important, assurances that the old "slaveocracy" of the antebellum period did not reassert itself through new means.

After disputes with Johnson over a Civil Rights Act and the reauthorization of the Freedmen's Bureau (both passed over his veto), Congress took the revolutionary steps included in the Reconstruction Acts. The legislation settled the philosophical debate over whether former Confederates had actually seceded. Abraham Lincoln had argued that secession was impossible and thus that the states never truly left the union. The Reconstruction Acts established that the Confederate states were out of the union. In order to be readmitted, Congress required that southerners revise their state constitutions to include universal manhood suffrage and ratify the Fourteenth Amendment, which declared all people born or naturalized in the United States to be citizens (thus reversing the Dred Scott decision) and guaranteed their equal protection under the law. In the interim, state boundaries and institutions themselves disappeared. Military governors administered calls for representatives to state constitutional conventions and many of these conventions featured prominent participation by African Americans. Tennessee ratified the Fourteenth Amendment before passage of the Reconstruction Acts and, as a result, was spared inclusion in the military districts. In all other southern states, however, the slow process of constitutional reform proceeded. A remarkable feature of the process was the active participation by black men in the drafting of new state constitutions. By 1868, six of the states had finished and Congress approved their reentry. The remainder did so by 1870. This marked the official end of congressional control over Reconstruction, but the structures established under the acts, principally, black voting and the establishment of a viable southern wing of the Republican Party, ensured that radical Reconstruction would continue on the ground in the South. These new governments ruled for several years in most southern states, establishing the first systems of public education in the region, inaugurating railroad projects, and creating a bare minimum of protection for the civil and political rights of black citizens.

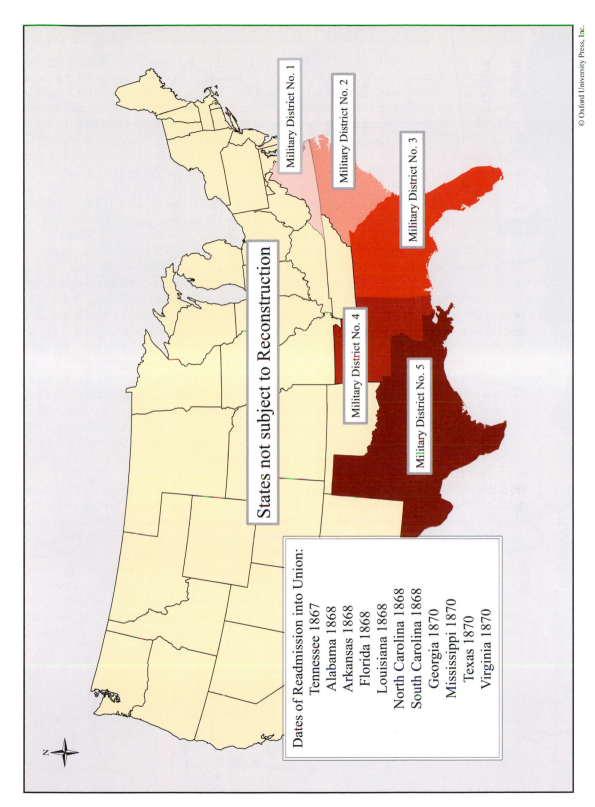

Military District No. 1

Military District No. 2

Military District No. 3

Military District No. 4

Military District No. 5

States not subject to Reconstruction

Dates of Readmission into Union:
Tennessee 1867
Alabama 1868
Arkansas 1868
Florida 1868
Louisiana 1868
North Carolina 1868
South Carolina 1868
Georgia 1870
Mississippi 1870
Texas 1870
Virginia 1870

N

When Andrew Johnson succeeded Lincoln as president in 1865, radical Republicans celebrated. Johnson, a Tennessee Democrat who remained loyal to the union, spoke of secession as treason and seemed sure to support radicals' efforts to break the power of the old slaveholding elite once and for all. Before the war, Johnson had been an ardent supporter of the average voter and a bitter enemy of planters. As it turned out, radicals came to despise Johnson for his uncharacteristic leniency with southern elites after the war. Johnson favored a quick Reconstruction and one conducted primarily by the states. Accordingly, he vetoed both the 1866 Civil Rights Act and the extension of the Freedmen's Bureau as unwarranted extensions of federal power. The Civil Rights Act, the first of its kind in U.S. history, would have guaranteed a bare minimum of what were at the time called "social rights": the right to marry and have control over one's children, the right to sue and be sued in federal court, and the right to own property. This was little more than what the Black Codes had promised but even this, backed as it was by federal authority, offended Johnson's small government ideals. So too with the Freedmen's Bureau, which was a time-limited agency staffed by only 900 agents to cover the entire South. Although demonized by ex-Confederates, the bureau actually provided valuable assistance to both blacks and whites, especially in its distribution of rations during the desperate winter of 1865–1866 and its work building schools.

The vote to overturn Johnson's veto of the 1866 Civil Rights Act showed the support at that time for a more aggressive Reconstruction and one in which the federal government would play a larger role. The defection of numerous border state Republicans and Democratic solidarity in sustaining the veto produced a map that more closely resembled the pattern of political support after the 1862 midterm elections than it did the electoral map of 1864, which sent the congressmen who voted on the measure. Border state congressmen, including representatives of Missouri, Kentucky, and Maryland, as well as lower North members from southern Illinois, southern Pennsylvania, and southern New York/New Jersey all supported Johnson, some no doubt from an ideological predisposition to limited government and others out of animosity to any measure that helped the freedmen. Several state legislatures, including Minnesota and Connecticut, also expressed their opposition to the measure.

The conflict between Johnson and congressional Republicans led to a rupture between the two branches of government. Johnson traveled the country, speaking out against passage of the Fourteenth Amendment, a cornerstone of congressional Reconstruction. With aggressive use of federal purse strings and its statutory authority, Congress substantially reduced Johnson's role in Reconstruction, but the disputes between liberals and conservatives over the proper role of the federal government in protecting individual rights in the United States did not abate. When white southerners organized the Ku Klux Klan as a way to curtail the freedom of African Americans, Congress responded with the Force Acts of 1870 and 1871. These measures increased federal authority by making it a crime to deny someone's civil rights, as in the exercise of the vote. They also empowered the new Justice Department to target the Klan, which it did successfully, arresting thousands of individuals associated with America's first domestic terrorist organization.

Supported
Opposed
Abstained

Note: Eight Republicans — all but one border state representatives — voted against the measure. No Democrats supported it.

© Oxford University Press, Inc.

49 U.S. Congressional Elections

Northern voters supported the shift to a more radical Reconstruction, returning a Republican majority to Congress in 1866 and 1870, but this was not their only concern. The postwar Congresses were responsible for overseeing significant transformations in the national economy, the settlement of the West, the Plains Indian Wars, and more. Republicans performed most of these tasks adequately but the Democrats continued to rebuild their party after the setbacks of secession and Civil War. One of the Democrats' advantages turned out to be embarrassments of the Grant administration. Ulysses S. Grant was elected in 1868 to huge acclaim on the slogan "Let us have peace." Supporters hoped he would be another Washington, knitting the country together after the devastation of the war. Grant proved a failure as president, too trusting of aides who hedged or openly flouted the law in sordid personal deals and unable to shape the course of politics as he had the war. The administration was critically weakened by evidence of corruption, cronyism, and general incompetence.

The Grant administration eventually became a rallying point for disaffected Republicans, and in 1872, they launched a major challenge within their own party. The so-called "Liberal Republicans" (actually those ideologically closer to the conservative Democrats) broke with the administration and supported fusion or "independent" tickets that joined like-minded Republicans and Democrats who opposed present policies. This faction did not succeed in displacing Grant, but it did disorganize and weaken the Republican Party. Liberal Republicans drew support by combining the Democrats' white supremacist ideology with a call for an immediate end to Reconstruction. This policy resonated with northern voters increasingly unhappy with the continued expense and burden of regulating conditions in the South. Most northerners had been outraged at the actions of the Ku Klux Klan and equally concerned that Democratic lawmakers in most southern states seemed unwilling to prosecute the crimes they committed. But with the federal indictments of Klan leaders in 1871, many northerners felt it was time to let politics take its course. That this meant a return to a social order based on a violent white supremacy did not bother many weary white northerners. This shift could be seen in law as well. In 1877, the Supreme Court undermined the Fourteenth Amendment's protection of individual rights in the infamous *Cruikshank* decision, which set free the ringleaders of the brutal 1873 Colfax Massacre.

The shift of northern voters to the right, especially on the question of continuing Reconstruction, can be seen most clearly in the results from the 1874 midterm elections. Democrats regained fifty-four seats from Republicans and took control of the House of Representatives, which they had not held since before the war. In addition to controlling nearly all of the South, Democrats ran strongly all across the Lower North and even in parts of New England. Under Grant, the federal government continued to protect the rights of southern African Americans, but by 1875, even his administration recognized the new mandate. When Mississippi Republicans appealed for federal troops to suppress the white militia acting on behalf of conservative Democrats, the administration demurred. Southern Democrats had finally won their battle, partly through violence against Republicans, black and white, in the South, and partly through outlasting northern voters who, after four years of war and eight more years of Reconstruction, seemed ready to give up their quest to remake the South in the image of the North.

Note: Democrats defeated 54 Republican incumbents and controlled the House of Representatives, 176–106.

Republican
Democratic
Independent
Territories

50 SHARECROPPING IN THE UNITED STATES

One of the most important issues of Reconstruction was the future shape of the southern economy and its relation to the nation. In particular, the question of what role the freedmen would play vexed policymakers in both the North and South. Southern planters assumed that slaves would stay where they were and continue to do the work they had done for generations. Some even claimed to be glad of emancipation, for now planters were absolved of the responsibility of caring for elderly or disabled slaves. Most whites imagined blacks would come to be a peasant class, confined to the rural areas of the South. This was the result of emancipation in Brazil (which joined Cuba in freeing its slaves in the 1880s), but the unique political dynamics of the United States ensured that ex-slaves in North America would receive political rights that Brazilian freedmen did not earn for decades. The political enfranchisement of black Americans meant that the question of labor would never be left solely to the market.

In the immediate wake of emancipation, many freedpeople moved to cities. Some did so to escape a tyrannical master, others simply because they could. As one woman said, in reference to remaining on the plantation where she had been raised, "If I stay here, I'll never know I'm free." This process produced a labor glut in many southern cities. Places like New Orleans, Mobile, Charleston, and Savannah all received African American migrants despite populations already swollen by wartime movement. The result was a burgeoning population of poor, often unemployed, black southerners in the years immediately after the war. Eventually, many people, both black and white, were forced to return to the countryside to look for work.

The most notable change to the southern farm economy was the splintering of land ownership and the rise of sharecropping. In the antebellum South, large planters had consolidated their control of increasingly large farms. In many parts of the Cotton South, farms of 500 acres or more were the norm. Much of this land would have been fallow at any given time, but slaves could be shifted to perform different tasks on different plots, increasing the efficiency of the farm as a whole. In the postbellum world, few farmers could maintain holdings on the same scale. Southern farms were subdivided repeatedly over the coming generations, well past the point of efficiency, producing an average holding of only twenty-one acres by the time of the Great Depression. Concomitant with the subdivision of southern real estate was the rise of sharecropping. Today, this practice is uniformly regarded as a recipe for exploitation by the landowner, but its origins reveal a more complicated story. As one historian has described it, southern planters went from being labor-lords to landlords. After the war, if they were to prosper, they needed people working the land. African Americans knew how to farm but did not want to do so under the supervision of whites. By farming on shares—where a landless family would essentially borrow use of the land in exchange for half or more of the final crop—blacks achieved an important measure of autonomy. They could work when and how they liked; they could put their whole family to work in the field or just the men. Whatever the ultimate decisions they made, the crucial difference was that they made those decisions. For landholders, the key issue was that they were guaranteed some return. Problems developed as southern merchants increasingly demanded cotton for payment of debts. By the 1880s, an overreliance on cotton, with its unpredictable price shifts owing to changes in global supply and demand, and the structural inequities of the southern economic system, transformed sharecropping into a tool of exploitation that served the interests of white landowners, if not the region, well into the 1950s.

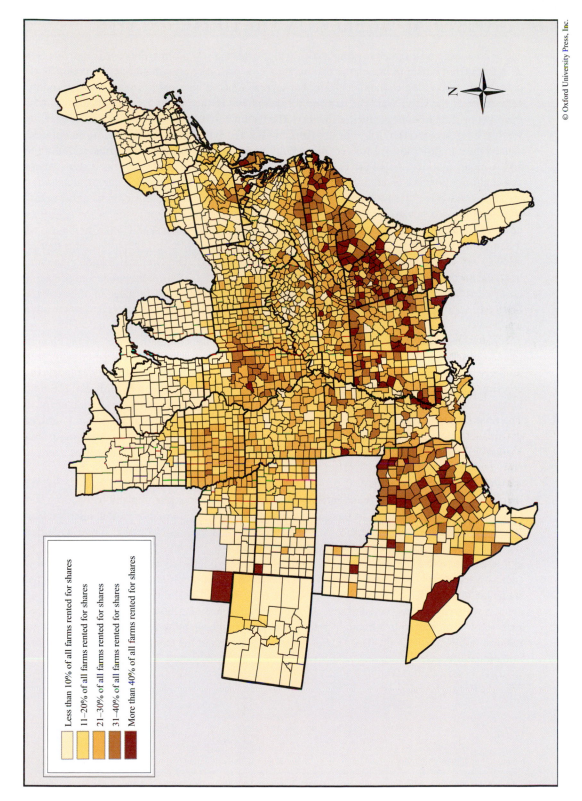

Less than 10% of all farms rented for shares
11–20% of all farms rented for shares
21–30% of all farms rented for shares
31–40% of all farms rented for shares
More than 40% of all farms rented for shares

51 INDUSTRIAL WORKERS IN THE UNITED STATES

As southerners struggled to rebuild their region after the war, northerners used the war as a platform from which to launch the nation into a new period of growth and development. This was particularly true in the economic sphere, but several areas of national life were restructured by the experience of the Civil War. The demand for manpower in the armies forced industries that relied upon young men to improve their efficiency. The nation's first assembly line (or, in this case, disassembly line) was pioneered by meatpackers in Chicago who saw a huge increase in demand for canned meat in order to feed soldiers in the field. Several of the meatpacking firms, including Swift and Armour, that dominated the economic life of the postbellum Midwest gained substantial size and sophistication as a result of the war. Typical war industries, like firearms, chemical manufacturers, and iron works, all saw booms, but the spur to development and innovation went beyond these staples. Railroads became an even more important factor in the economic life of the nation as the government came to rely upon them for the shipment of men and material. Unlike the South, where the rail lines were essentially nationalized, the North created public-private partnerships that paved the way for substantial postwar cooperation (for good and ill). The National Banking Act streamlined the northern economy, forcing the consolidation of the 7,000 different public and private institutions that had been issuing banknotes before the war. This change was initiated in order to ease the fiscal demands of the war, but the infrastructure remained in place and helped foster growth after the war as well.

The war did not by itself create industrial America, but the cumulative effect of the changes in finance, transportation, and manufacturing enabled real opportunities for industrial growth for those properly positioned. Almost all of this development occurred in the North and the result was the increasing concentration of factories and industrial work in the Northeast and Midwest. If the South lagged behind in terms of manufacturing establishments in 1860, the gap was even larger by 1880. The South's nearly exclusive focus on cotton production, the enormous capital deficit produced by the emancipation of slaves, and the heavy postwar investment in northern manufacturing produced a grossly unequal distribution of industrial facilities, the effects of which can still be seen in the early twenty-first century.

Another effect of the war was the shift in national attention from the South to the West. Where before the war, much political and intellectual energy was spent explaining and reconciling slavery and the slave-based economy of the South into the increasingly free-labor nation, after the war the nearly exclusive regional concern was America west of Kansas and Nebraska. White settlement of the Plains States was made possible by the Homestead Act, passed by the 37th Congress after the exit of the Southern Democrats who had long opposed such legislation. The United States won the Indian Wars of the 1870s and 1880s in part because it had a much larger, better-equipped, better-trained, and better-led force after the war than it had before. The military leaders of the campaigns against western Indians included several former Union generals, most famously William T. Sherman and Philip Sheridan. Although historians tend to emphasize the role of Reconstruction in the nation's political life for the decade after the war, the effects of the Civil War were felt in every area of national life.

Less than 100 industrial workers

100–1,000 industrial workers

1,001–10,000 industrial workers

10,001–220,000 industrial workers

Note: Tabulation includes both male and female workers. Scale increases exponentially.

52 | U.S. PRESIDENTIAL ELECTION

Historians traditionally regard 1877 as the end of Reconstruction. By that year, Democratic governments ruled all the former Confederate states and the last U.S. troops stationed in the South had been recalled. Those who celebrated this reversal referred to it as "redemption," adopting a deliberately Christian concept to describe their deliverance out of their suffering under Republicans. In fact, Democrats had gained control of most state governments well before 1877. Likewise, the vast majority of U.S. troops had been decommissioned in 1865. Whenever it occurred, the reestablishment of Democratic Party rule ushered in an era of single-party government that lasted in the American South, in many places, into the second half of the twentieth century. Democrats regained control through the use of violence, either in official alliance with the Ku Klux Klan or through unofficial alliances with white "militias," directed against Republican, and, in particular, African American officeholders. They also remobilized white voters who had abandoned politics with the rise of Republican state governments in the South. Democrats campaigned against the new taxes imposed by Republican governments that funded broad-based and popular programs like public education as well as the usually unsuccessful and frequently corrupt alliances with railroad companies. The combination of effective politics and outright violence that propelled Democrats to victory in the late 1870s ushered in several generations of state policies organized around the principles of white supremacy.

1877 is also infamous because it was the year that Rutherford B. Hayes, an Ohio Republican and Union general in the Civil War, won the presidency over Samuel Tilden, a New York Democrat. The outcome of the presidential contest was intimately tied to the fate of Republican governments in the South. Tilden won the popular vote and but for contested votes from three crucial states (Florida, South Carolina, and Louisiana), would have secured an electoral college victory as well. Both sides bitterly disputed the proper attribution of votes and the conflict dragged on into the winter, with partisans on both sides threatening a return to Civil War. Democratic and Republican negotiators eventually reached a settlement that granted Republicans the White House (which they would hold, with the exception of Grover Cleveland's and Woodrow Wilson's terms in office, until 1932) and released state control back to Democrats. Negotiated partly through intermediaries who were themselves major players in the emerging contest for control of the transcontinental railroad lines, the "corrupt bargain" signaled the final capitulation from northern whites on the issue of race relations in the Old South.

Tilden drew considerable strength outside the South, including such northern states as Indiana, Connecticut, New Jersey, and New York. The Republicans, in contrast, dominated the North and West. Republican control of the White House and Congress for much of the next generation depended on this regional distribution; they focused their efforts on the populous urban areas in the North and on the rapidly expanding western frontier. Though competitive at the state level in some Upper South states, the Republicans had little presence in the Deep South. Democrats, in contrast, ruled supreme over much of the South until the 1950s, when the party split, as whites moved increasingly into the Republican Party. Democrats also contested Republican dominance in many northern places, particularly cities. The changes wrought by the Civil War were also felt beyond politics. By confirming the perpetuity of the union and by destroying slavery, the war fundamentally altered the shape and future of the United States.

N

Supported Tilden (Democrat)
Supported Hayes (Republican)
No Vote (Territories)

Maine
Vermont
New Hampshire
Massachusetts
Connecticut
New York
Rhode Island
New Jersey
Pennsylvania
Maryland
Delaware
West Virginia
Virginia
Ohio
Kentucky
North Carolina
South Carolina
Tennessee
Georgia
Florida
Indiana
Alabama
Illinois
Mississippi
Michigan
Wisconsin
Missouri
Arkansas
Louisiana
Iowa
Minnesota
Dakota Territory
Nebraska
Kansas
Oklahoma
Texas
Colorado
Wyoming
New Mexico
Montana
Utah
Arizona
Idaho
Nevada
Washington
Oregon
California

Reassertion of Democratic Party Rule:
Virginia 1869
North Carolina 1870
Georgia 1871
Texas 1873
Alabama 1874
Arkansas 1874
Mississippi 1876
South Carolina 1876
Florida 1877
Louisiana 1877

SELECTED BIBLIOGRAPHY

Geographic Sources

Louisiana State University Geoscience Publications. *Historical United States County Boundary Files, 1790–1999,* 1999.

National Atlas of the United States, 200512, Streams and Waterbodies of the United States: National Atlas of the United States, Reston, VA. <http://nationalatlas.gov/atlasftp.html> Downloaded August 10, 2006.

USGS National Center for EROS, 200509, Grayscale North America Shaded Relief—1-Kilometer Resolution: National Atlas of the United States, Reston, VA. <http://nationalatlas.gov/atlasftp.html> Downloaded August 10, 2006.

Primary Sources

Appleton's Annual Cyclopedia and Register of Important Events. New York: D. Appleton, 1861–1879.

Basler, Roy P. *Collected Works of Abraham Lincoln.* New Brunswick, NJ: Rutgers University Press, 1953–1955.

Berlin, Ira, Thavolia Glymph, Steven F. Miller, Joseph P. Reidy, and Julie Saville. *Freedom.* Vol. 3, Series 1, *The Wartime Genesis of Free Labor: The Lower South: A Documentary History of Emancipation, 1861–1867.* Cambridge: Cambridge University Press, 1991.

Berlin, Ira, Steven F. Miller, Joseph P. Reidy, and Leslie S. Rowland. *Freedom.* Vol. 2, Series 1, *The Wartime Genesis of Free Labor: The Upper South: A Documentary History of Emancipation, 1861–1867.* Cambridge: Cambridge University Press, 1993.

Journals of the Congress of the Confederate States of America, 1861–1865. Vols. 2–7. Washington, DC: Senate Document No. 234, *U.S. Serial Set,* 58th Congress, 2nd session, 1904–1905.

U.S. Bureau of the Census. *Eighth Census of the United States, 1860.* 4 vols. Washington, DC: Government Printing Office, 1865.

U.S. Congress. *Congressional Globe.* 37th–39th Congresses, 1861–1867.

U.S. War Department. *The War of Rebellion: A Compilation of the Official Records of the Union and Confederate Armies.* 127 vols., index, and atlas. Washington, DC: Government Printing Office, 1880–1901.

U.S. War Department, George B. Davis, Leslie J. Perry, Joseph W. Kirkley, and Calvin D. Cowles. *The Official Military Atlas of the Civil War.* 1895. Reprint, New York: Barnes & Noble, 2003.

Secondary Sources

Alexander, Thomas B., and Richard E. Beringer. *The Anatomy of the Confederate Congress: A Study of the Influences of Member Characteristics on Legislative Voting Behavior, 1861–1865.* Nashville, TN: Vanderbilt University Press, 1972.

Ash, Stephen. *When the Yankees Came: Conflict & Chaos in the Occupied South.* Chapel Hill: University of North Carolina Press, 1995.

Ball, Douglas B. *Financial Failure and Confederate Defeat.* Urbana: University of Illinois Press, 1991.

Ballard, Michael. *Vicksburg: The Campaign that Opened the Mississippi.* Chapel Hill: University of North Carolina Press, 2004.

Bensel, Richard Franklin. *Yankee Leviathan: The Origins of Central State Authority in America, 1859–1877.* Cambridge: Cambridge University Press, 1990.

Black, Robert C., III. *The Railroads of the Confederacy.* Chapel Hill: University of North Carolina Press, 1952.

Bynum, Victoria. *The Free State of Jones: Mississippi's Longest Civil War.* Chapel Hill: University of North Carolina Press, 2001.

Daniel, Larry J. *Shiloh: The Battle that Changed the Civil War.* New York: Simon & Schuster, 1997.

Dotson, Rand. "'The Grave and Scandalous Evil Infected To Your People:' The Erosion of Confederate Loyalty in Floyd County, Virginia." V*irginia Magazine of History and Biography*, 2000 (Vol. 108, no. 4): 393–434.

Dubin, Michael J. *United States Presidential Elections, 1788–1860: The Official Results by County and State.* Jefferson, NC: McFarland and Co., 2002.

———. *United States Congressional Elections, 1788–1997: The Official Results of the Elections of the 1st through 105th Congresses.* Jefferson, NC: McFarland and Co, 1998.

Fisher, Noel C. *War at Every Door: Partisan Politics and Guerrilla Violence in East Tennessee, 1860–1869.* Chapel Hill: University of North Carolina Press, 1997.

Gallagher, Gary W., ed. *Chancellorsville: The Battle and Its Aftermath.* Chapel Hill: University of North Carolina Press, 1996.

Geary, James W. *We Need Men: The Union Draft in the Civil War.* DeKalb: Northern Illinois University Press, 1991.

Gerteis, Louis S. *From Contraband to Freedman: Federal Policy Toward Southern Blacks, 1861–1865.* Westport, CT: Greenwood Press, 1973.

Griess, Thomas E. *Atlas for the American Civil War.* Wayne, NJ: Avery Publishing Group, 1986.

Hennessy, John J. *Return to Bull Run: The Battle and Campaign of Second Manassas.* Norman: University of Oklahoma Press, 1999.

Martis, Kenneth C. *The Historical Atlas of United States Congressional Districts, 1789–1983.* New York: Free Press, 1982.

———. *The Historical Atlas of Political Parties in the United States Congress 1789–1989.* New York: Macmillan, 1989.

———. *The Historical Atlas of the Congresses of the Confederate States of America, 1861–1865.* New York: Simon & Schuster, 1994.

McFeely, William S. *Yankee Stepfather: General O.O. Howard and the Freedmen.* New Haven, CT: Yale University Press, 1968.

McMurry, Richard M. *Atlanta, 1864: Last Chance for the Confederacy.* Lincoln: University of Nebraska Press, 2000.

McPherson, James M., ed. *The Atlas of the Civil War*. New York: Macmillan, 1994.

———. *Battle Cry of Freedom: The Civil War Era*. New York: Oxford University Press, 1988.

———. *Ordeal by Fire: The Civil War and Reconstruction*. 3rd ed. New York: McGraw Hill, 2001.

Meinig, D. W. *The Shaping of America: A Geographical Perspective on 500 Years of History*. Vol. 2; *Continental America, 1800–1867*. New Haven, CT: Yale University Press, 1993.

Moore, Albert Burton. *Conscription and Conflict in the Confederacy*. New York: Macmillan, 1924.

Neely, Mark E. *The Fate of Liberty: Abraham Lincoln and Civil Liberties*. New York: Oxford University Press, 1991.

———. *Southern Rights: Political Prisoners and the Myth of Confederate Constitutionalism*. Charlottesville: University Press of Virginia, 1999.

Phillips, David. *Maps of the Civil War: The Roads They Took*. New York: Friedman/Fairfax, 1998.

Rable, George. *The Confederate Republic: A Revolution Against Politics*. Chapel Hill: University of North Carolina Press, 1994.

———. *Fredericksburg! Fredericksburg!* Chapel Hill: University of North Carolina Press, 2002.

Randall, J. G. *The Civil War and Reconstruction*. Boston: D.C. Heath, 1937.

———. *Constitutional Problems Under Lincoln*. Urbana: Univ. of Illinois Press, 1951.

Roberts, William H. *Now for the Contest: Coastal and Oceanic Naval Operations in the Civil War*. Lincoln: University of Nebraska Press, 2004.

Sears, Stephen W. *Landscape Turned Red: The Battle of Antietam*. New York: Ticknor and Fields, 1983.

———. *To the Gates of Richmond: The Peninsula Campaign*. New York: Ticknor and Fields, 1992.

———. *Chancellorsville*. Boston: Houghton Mifflin, 1996.

———. *Gettysburg*. Boston: Houghton Mifflin, 2003.

Swanson, Mark. *Atlas of the Civil War, Month by Month: Major Battles and Troop Movements*. Athens: University of Georgia Press, 2004.

Symonds, Craig L. *A Battlefield Atlas of the Civil War*. Baltimore: The Nautical and Aviation Publishing Company of America, 1983.

Tanner, Robert. *Stonewall in the Valley: Thomas J. 'Stonewall' Jackson's Shenandoah Valley Campaign, Spring 1862*. Garden City, NJ: Doubleday, 1976.

Todd, Richard Cecil. *Confederate Finance*. Athens: University of Georgia Press, 1954.

Warner, Ezra J., and W. Buck Yearns. *Biographical Register of the Confederate Congress*. Baton Rouge: Louisiana State University Press, 1975.

Wiley, Bell Irvin. *Southern Negroes, 1861–1865*. Baton Rouge: Louisiana State University Press, 1965; 1938.

Woodhead, Henry, ed. *The Battle Atlas of the Civil War*. Alexandria, VA: Time-Life, 1991.

Wooster, Ralph A. *The Secession Conventions of the South*. Princeton, NJ: Princeton University Press, 1962.

Index